Vintage Laptop Computers
First Decade: 1980-89

A comprehensive collection of known, portable, self-contained travel computers that changed the way we live.

James E. Wilson

Outskirts Press, Inc.
Denver, Colorado

Vintage Laptop Computers
First Decade: 1980-89
All Rights Reserved
Copyright © 2006 James E. Wilson

Outskirts Press
http://www.outskirtspress.com

ISBN-10: 1-59800-489-1
ISBN-13: 978-1-59800-489-2

Library of Congress Control Number: 2006926844

Outskirts Press and the "OP" logo are trademarks belonging to
Outskirts Press, Inc.

Printed in the United States of America

Vintage Laptop Computers
First Decade: 1980-89

They Unchained Us

James E. Wilson

Acknowledgements

Writing a book was a completely different venture for me. One does not really know where to start as it is an endeavor of trial & error. A person needs help in almost every aspect of writing a manuscript the first time. You have to rely on family and friends to sometimes point you in the right direction.

I am grateful to my wife Laurel for her invaluable assistance in writing this book in terms of support, spelling, English, and terminology. I want to thank her for allowing me to spend the hundreds upon hundreds of hours devoted researching, purchasing, photographing, and assembling the information needed. Appreciation also goes to my daughters Barb and Sherrie, and my grandson Cody for their input.

And finally, many thanks to my collector-friend Sylvain Bizoirre at Old-Computers.Com Museum for assistance in putting this book together. Sylvain graciously permitted me to use their images of computers I do not collect, but needed for this book. Also of laptops I collect, but do not own. The input is greatly appreciated.

Acknowledgements

Dedicated to the 8 year quest for the acquisition and preservation of an example of all major laptop models from every manufacturer which produced them during the 1980s. Reconstructing the period that gave the world the luxury of mobile, self-contained computers for people on the go. To be able to do business anytime, anyplace, anywhere. I hope the readers will find my research and diligent efforts pleasurable, informative & rewarding.

Introduction

When researching and then writing a book on a specific topic, one must face the fact that some one may not agree with everything you have to say on the subject. With that said, they are free to tackle the project and print their own ideas just as I have.

My inspiration for writing this book is the hope it will bring back fond memories for the fortunate few who were lucky enough to possess "laptop" computers in their infancy. Also, to enlighten the unfortunate masses of us who never had the chance to view the travel computers which were available in the early years.

I can not remember if I even knew personal computers (let alone "laptops") existed during the 1980s. I was the owner of a small business keeping records and inventory on paper. I do not recall ever seeing laptops. To envision at the time that personal computers would have such a stranglehold on the way we did business by the end of the following decade would have been considered a "pipedream". The first time I remember seeing a PC was around 1990 when my daughter bought an Apple "Mac". I thought at the time, "Why would anyone want to mess around with that funny little box"? Well, by the end of 1993 I had purchased one of those "funny little boxes". Wow, what a speed demon--486 CPU, 33MHZ, 4 Megs of RAM, and Windows 3.1! I was on my first journey toward the outer limits of "Cyber Space". My life has never been the same!

I have labored many, many hours over the past 8 years searching through magazines and their ads, online auctions, newspapers, websites, operating and service manuals, and anywhere else I could find a tidbit of information about "laptops". This has definitely been a labor of love. I feel this book contains a wealth of data on all known "laptop" computers I have found to exist in the 1980s. The biggest percentage of "laptops" you see in this book I have personally collected, all are still in operable condition. Some of the information shown has been retrieved from them. I have included both my own "laptops" and the ones I have not yet acquired with specifications, images, and thumb nail sketches of each unit to provide a good overview of these early models.

Table of Contents

Table of Contents (cont'd)

Table of Contents (cont'd)

What is a Laptop…???

Defining the difference between various types of personal computers produced during the 1980s was not always as black and white as it is today. Now there is no problem determining the difference between a "laptop" and "desktop" computer. Early computers were designed in a countless array of shapes, sizes, and different types, and appeared to merge together in many ways. Computer types were called names like lunch box, professional, luggable, pocket, MSX, suitcase, transportable, laptop, and home computer. From what I can interpret, the term "laptop" is probably a misnomer as the term came about when someone said "this portable is designed in a shape that can be placed on your lap", and the name stuck. In the early days of personal computers this machine was not marketed as a "laptop", it was just another type of portable computer.

During my years of research I have come to believe the term "laptop" in the early days, to be in the eye of the beholder. I guess you could say I have formed one man's opinion on the subject-mine. This collection of "laptops" I have acquired reflects my definition of what should be deemed a "laptop" computer. I believe the unit has to be small enough-the size of a sheet of paper or a little larger, light enough-below 15lbs, and will sit on your lap. It has to be all in one piece and be able to operate under its own power supply. Others may have opposing criteria but to my knowledge no one has published any different ideas. I also have what I call a "cross-over" section of computers in the collection. These units have the shape of a laptop but are a bit heavy, too large, too small, or do not have the required functions to be called "laptop". You can see it is hard to draw the line. Until someone, who is more knowledgeable than myself, can come up with a better way of defining the difference and publishes a more comprehensive work, I consider this book to be the most complete and accurate offering of information on vintage "laptop" computers in print.

Are You Wondering...?
& Other Tidbits

You are probably questioning my sanity in collecting these old relics. It all started when I received a Compaq LTE 8086 in a group of laptops several years ago and was amazed by how "old" it looked. It was actually only 10 years old! Early "laptops" are at most 25 years old, but relatively speaking, I consider them as antiquated as the telegraph and Indian smoke signals, but these two means of communication are over 140 years old.

That sparked my interest and I started researching "laptops". I soon discovered very few were manufactured in the 1980s. So, I started buying up what I considered to be "a laptop" whenever one became available. Then, I thought it would be great to get an example from each company, and---well, why not try to get an example of every major model from each company! The rest, as they say, is history.

I was amazed and intrigued at the variance in the shapes and sizes of laptops during that era. It was as if someone said, holding their hands apart, "take a case this big, hinge a display on the top and build a laptop out of it". It looked as though, with a couple of exceptions, nobody was looking at what other companies were producing. The shapes that some came up with were astounding. The sizes varied from 7"x10"x2" to 16"x22"x4", and weights varied between 3lbs and 20lbs. The first laptops had one trait in common. All of the early ones (with the exception of the "A4" types, which had open displays) had the displays hinged in the middle of the unit top. The display slanted downward to the front. As the screens became larger manufacturers started to hinge them in the back. The displays of the era were thick and bulky and screens came in many colors-black, grey, green, yellow, blue, and orange. The text was different colors also, to contrast with the background for improved viewing. Mono LCD and gas plasma screens were difficult to read, especially when viewed at an angle and in certain lighting conditions as very few displays were backlit.

Many feel the Epson HX-20 to be the first laptop (circa 1982) and the Grid Compass 1101 the first "clamshell" laptop (1982). The best known was the Tandy Model 100. It was a favorite with newspaper men all over the world. The 100 was a spin-off of the Kyotronic 85 as were Olivetti M10, and NEC 8201A. All were basically the same unit with a few modifications. The most popular "laptop" type was the "clamshell design" after which all modern laptops are patterned. Unlike the "cookie cutter" appearance of computers today, the earliest machines came in many shapes, forms, and colors. Almost all early models had Intel 8086 & 8088, Zilog Z80 or NEC V20/30 CPUs, all were conceived in the latter part of the 1970s, or early 80s.

Motorola/Hitachi also made chips during the same era. By 1986, a few laptops had Intel 80286 CPUs, (which was very late as this processor was introduced in 1982), and a hard drive installed. To date I have discovered 87 major models built by 42 different companies.

I estimate there may be as many as 50 companies who produced laptops, and up to 100 major models built by them during the 1980s using my ratio of discovery over the last 8 years of research. There must be few unknown manufacturers who built laptops, plus a few different models of known companies that have yet to be unearthed from their deep, dark, hiding places.

Computer collectors today seem to have more interest in early laptops than in the past. This is probably due to the impact they have had on our society, and their availability. It's hard to imagine these not being available when traveling, be it in a motel room, or on an airplane. It appears to me prices have risen, and the supply of rare units, have dropped, over the last couple of years as collectors snap up hard-to-find laptops. There are approximately 20 manufacturers and 30 models built which are extremely difficult to locate, and for a select few, very costly. Also, it should be noted that many manufacturers and common models are very plentiful, with little value. I believe the few enlightened souls who collect scarce laptops today will have some very treasured items in the not so distant future.

Very few vintage laptops have the manuals/documentation which came with them when they were sold. This makes attempting to operate an old laptop, or finding any information on doing so, a real problem. This also creates a challenge when trying to power them up. Some have buttons & slides, others have on/off switches, or rocker switches on the side, some are located on the back, others are on the inside, while a few have none! The "Gavilan" powers on by pushing both the control keys down at the same time. "Psion" starts by pressing the "Psion" key + the esc key, and shuts down by pressing the Ctrl key + the Psion" key + the #1 key. Try figuring that one out without a manual! The "Kaypro 2000" turns on/off by simply opening and closing the display. So you can see the problems facing you in getting a machine to perform as it was intended. Besides that, very few people know, or knew then, how to use the old operating systems installed in laptops in those early days.

"Laptop" computers were not overly popular during the 80s due to high prices, and for most units, not having the latest technology. There were a few exceptions to this, for example, the Tandy TRS 80 Model 100 was a wildly popular unit, thanks to its size, weight, and cost. There were a few other laptops that did fairly well, but overall, laptops were produced in very small numbers as there was little demand. That makes some brands very difficult, or impossible to locate.

Some of us have cars, stoves, refrigerators, TV's, etc, which are 20-30 years old, or older, and still serve us almost as flawlessly as new ones. However, I consider today's 10 year old computers essentially obsolete, due to advancements in software, or internal hardware. Never before has an industry been able to render a machine completely useless in such a short amount of time.

Manufacturers have learned that by building new models monthly, or sooner, and by changing software, they are able to harvest gigantic amounts of revenue, as computer "geeks" must always possess the latest technology available.

There are three laptops in the collection not produced in the 1980s, the "Dell 316LT" (1990), the "Apple Macintosh Powerbook 100" (1991), and the "Gateway 2000 Handbook" (1993). I feel the first laptops built by these industry leaders should have a place in a vintage "laptop" collection.

Three things still completely baffle me: 1. I have heard of a computer "expert" making the remark, "a 20 meg hard drive, you will never fill that up". 2. How could anyone ever design a small ½" chip that would store all the information printed in a library, and more?? 3. 60 years ago it was quoted by a business person talking about computers, "someday there may be a need for about fifty of these things"!

Until someone, (like me) publishes a book containing information, photos, and specifications of these old beauties, I believe they will remain in the "dark ages" of cyber space.

Transitional Laptops &...

When did the "old" stop and the "new" begin? This seems to be a popular question. The Intel 80286 CPU and/or the internal hard drive were first installed in a "laptop", circa 1986, in the "Gridcase 1520", and Toshiba T-3100". Toshiba and Grid were way ahead of most companies as none of the other manufacturers of laptops had 80286 CPU's or hard drives until circa 1988. Some computers used floppies and cassette tapes for data storage into the 1990's, i.e. "Armstrad NC-100".

As it occurs today, the latest CPU's, hard drives, and RAM, always lag behind the desktops by a couple of years before being installed in laptops, likewise with the operating systems. Intel's 80286 CPU's and hard drives were installed in "luggable" and "lunch-box" computers beginning in the middle 80s. Windows was conceived in 1983 and installed in portables in 1985 as Windows 1.0 and used as a front-in for DOS. Windows of this era was not a "stand alone" operating system. From what I can gather it took at least an 80286 CPU to run the operating system, therefore they would not be installed in laptops until later. This was probably for the best as Windows of that time (Versions 1.0 and 2.0) were not "user friendly" systems. Not until Version 3.0 was released in1990 was there an easy-to-use Windows Operating System. There were several different operating systems used during the decade, with "DOS" being the dominant one. CGA color displays were beginning to be used in laptops during the late 80s as was an occasional 80386 CPU (1989).

About the time the Windows operating system was being introduced into the laptop line, another earth shaking advancement was on the horizon: "networking"; an idea of connecting computers together. All of a sudden personal computers were taken out of the home and brought together in a global network. The business and personal world was at our fingertips. Civilization would never be the same again!

There was also a trend in the late 80s toward much smaller and lighter laptops, i.e. the NEC "Ultralite" and Zenith "Minisport" at about 5lbs. There is always a trade-off in doing this, smaller units, smaller displays. There were still big heavy (15lb) clunkers with old CPU's, or no hard drives, produced into the next decade.

So the point of this discussion, where do you cut off collecting the first "decade" of laptops? I surmised 1990 would be the logical point. It seemed to be the midpoint between the "new" and "old" in regards to faster CPU's, more RAM, internal hard drives, and the now dominant Windows Operating System.

The1980s were very turbulent years in the fast moving new personal computer market. Companies and individuals jockeyed for position, there were numerous lawsuits over infringements, innovations, and patents, etc. Many companies started up and failed. People were switching from one company to another, or starting their own.

Many new products and ideas were introduced, a few did succeed, but most didn't, and many good ideas were bought up by larger companies. It was definitely a "dog, eat dog" era. Only the strong survived!!

There were a couple of laptops built in the late 1980s included in the collection which have the "new" technology—80286 chip and/or a hard drive. These were used as stepping stones to the modern laptops we know today.

Information Accuracy

The information on the laptop computers in this collection has been gathered from many different sources. It came from the manufacturer's manuals, from my research, the laptops themselves, and the rest is more or less educated guesswork. The accuracy of some information collected may be questionable. For example, in one instance I found four different answers, from four different sources, on the same topic. I reviewed the accrued info and tried to come up with a consensus realizing that accurate answers from some manufacturers were virtually unobtainable. I have found little or no data anywhere on many of these laptops. The specifications and thumb nail descriptions shown on the following pages contain all pertinent information that I was able to uncover. I feel this group of computers I have accumulated is probably one of the finest and most complete collections of 1980's laptops in existence.

This book is written in laymen's terms. I am not a computer "nerd" or guru so some technical terms may be over-simplified. Although I have been a collector of vintage "laptops" for over 8 years, I am not an authority on the workings of these great old "paperweights". The statements and views are my opinions, and may or may not be 100% correct. I have tried to be as accurate as possible using the data I had available.

So, in closing, take this information with a "grain of salt", and use it as a guide, not the Bible.

Values of Vintage Laptops...?

This is an oft-asked question. I have toyed with the idea of trying to come up with a list of values of individual laptops but I decided against it. I believe that it is impossible to achieve accurate values considering all the elements involved. How do you place a value on a certain laptop when there has only been 1 or 2 for sale in the last five years? There are factors that enter into value besides rarity, the condition, and is it operable? Does it have all the manuals or documentation that came with it when new? What about software, operating disc, and a power supply? Very few become available with all the above items. Probably less than 20% of laptops I have seen contain manuals and disc, and about 50% come with a power supply. Therefore, I assume only about half of the laptops for sale have been tested before you buy them--not a good average. Most people including myself do not know how to run the old operating systems. So, one of my criteria when buying a laptop is that it powers up, and the operating system boots, showing it could possibly operate as expected.

As I stated above, there is really little correlation between rarity and value. I have purchased several laptops which have been the only one of that particular type for sale at the time. One model, the Sharp PC-5500, I purchased for $16.00 including shipping, where another laptop in which there have been a great number available i.e. Tandy TRS-80 Model 100 sell for $60.00. The Tandy 100 is, for example, an exception to this rule. I have seen a laptop sell for $8.00, a few weeks later the same type sold for $50.00. What does that tell you? You can see why I have dropped the idea of a value list that could be anywhere near accurate.

In conclusion, I have decided that value is in the eye of the individual buyer, what he is willing to pay for a particular laptop, at a particular time, and at a particular place.

Rarity Scale

I am trying to fathom some semblance of a rarity scale to define the scarcity of laptop computers. This is just one man's opinion taken from my 8 years of research on the subject. My accuracy is anybody's guess. I felt the only viable basis available for compiling a workable scale was to count laptops which had been in auction listings or ads. I have seen images of units listed in collections/museums but a large percentage of those pictures have been of the same laptop. I do not consider them a reliable source. No one knows what may be long-since lost or hidden away in dark, secret places. We had to average the units that appeared in the marketplace over the above mentioned time span, to hopefully determine a usable scale.

So, with what we have to work with: HERE WE GO:

RARE: **0-4 pieces**

SCARCE: **5-12 pieces**

COMMON: **13-25 pieces**

PLENTIFUL: **Over 25 pieces**

Manufacturers of Pre 1990's Laptops

Company	Major Models Built	Origin
Ampere	(1)	Japan
Armstrad	(1)	UK
Bondwell	(3)	Hong Kong/US
Bull	(2)	Japan/France
Cambridge	(1)	Scotland
Casio	(1)	Japan/US
Commodore	(1)	US
Compaq	(1)	US
Compudata (Tulip)	(1)	Netherlands
Convergent Tech	(1)	US
Data General	(2)	US
Datavue	(2)	Japan/US
Dulmont	(1)	Australia
Epson	(5)	Japan/US
Ericsson	(1)	Sweden
Fujitsu	(1)	Japan
Gavilan	(1)	US
Grid	(5)	US
Hewlett-Packard	(1)	US
Hyundai	(1)	Korea/US
IBM	(2)	US
Kyocera	(1)	Japan/US
KayPro	(1)	US
Matsushita (Panasonic)	(2)	Japan/US
MicroOffice Systems	(1)	US
Laser	(1)	US
NEC	(5)	Japan/US
Olivitti	(2)	Italy/US
Psion	(3)	UK
Sanyo	(1)	Japan/US
Sharp	(6)	Japan/US
Sony	(1)	Japan/US
Sord	(2)	Japan:
Tandy	(5)	Japan/US

Tava	(1)	Japan/US
Teleram	(1)	US
Texas Instruments	(2)	US
Toshiba	(6)	Japan/US
Visual Technology	(1)	US
Wang	(1)	US
Xerox	(1)	US
Zenith	(5)	US

Other Known Models

These models are virtually, or exactly like, the collection models in appearance, but differ due to the following features:

(a) CPU, (b) RAM, (c) Display, (d) Bits, (e) Hard Drive

Collection Model	Other Models	Features
Galivan: 8 Bit	Gavilan 16 Bit	(d)
Grid Compass 1101	1102,07,09,29,37,39	(a) (b) (c)
Grid Grid Lite	Grid Lite Plus, XL	(c)
Gridcase 3	Gridcase 1, 2, & 4	(c) (e)
HP 110 45711B	45711A,C,D,E	(b)
NEC 8201A	8300	(b)
NEC Ultra Lite17-02	17-01	(e)
Psion MC400	MC600	(a) (c)
Sharp PC-4501	PC-4500	
Sharp PC-4600	PC-4601, 4641	
Tandy Model 80	TRS 100 TRS 102	(b)
Tandy 1100HD	1100FD	
Toshiba T-3100	3100e, SX, 20	(a) (b) (e)
Toshiba T1000	T-1000 LE, XE	(b) (c)
Toshiba T-1100 Plus	T-1100	
Toshiba T-1200XE	T1200, LE	(b)
Xerox 1800	1805 1810 1815	
Zenith ZFL 181-93	ZFL181-92, 181-97	
Zenith ZWL 184-02	ZWL 184-97	

1980-89:
First Decade of PC's

On the following pages are examples of different types of personal computers (other than laptops) built by over 300 companies during the 1980s. Included in this group is the Professional Computer which in both theory and appearance to be pretty much like the modern desktop, with the CPU case, the monitor, and keyboard in individual pieces. I feel portable computers should be classified in five main groups. The "Laptop" - a self contained unit with the CPU, keyboard, and monitor all in one piece. There were two styles of "laptops", the "open display or A4" type, and the "clamshell" type. These had their own power supply, were small enough, and light enough, to be placed on your lap to operate. The "Home Computer" type--hundreds of models were built in the 1980s, none of them (I have found) contained onboard displays. This type I consider to be antiquated, they had to be connected to a TV monitor for viewing. The "Luggable"-- were heavy units with many clones and look-a-likes. The "Lunchbox"-- portable, but heavier and larger than a laptop and was not all in one piece, they did not have their own power supply. The "Pocket" or handheld type--these contained their own power supply (battery). They were a small design with few features, most looked pretty similar but were too small to be considered a laptop. The last four types listed should not be classified as true "laptops" due to size, weight, or lacking required features.

This is probably one of my most controversial sections as some who have their own opinion on the subject will disagree with my interpretation. But, as I have previously stated, this is my own personal opinion on the topic. This can never be a cut & dried or a black and white subject!

Home Computer Type
(Needs TV Monitor)

Pocket (Hand held) Computers

Lunchbox Computers (Under 25#)

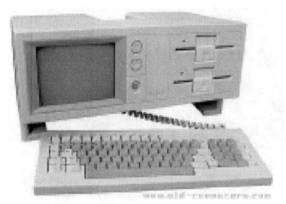

Luggable Computers (Over 25#)

Unusual Style Computers

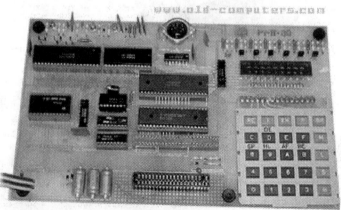

Professional Computers

Known Vintage Laptops

Rarity Scale

0-4 Rare	5 -12 Scarce	13-25 Common	Over 25 Plentiful
Display Type:	A4 -	Open Display	CS - Clamshell

Indicates in Collection

Ampere WS 1	1985	CS	Rare
Amstrad PPC 640	1988	CS	Common
Apple Macintosh PB 100	1991	CS	Common
Bondwell Model B2	1985	CS	Rare
Bondwell Pro 8T	1988	CS	Rare
Bondwell B200A	1988	CS	Scarce
Bull Honeywell SX-L	1989	CS	Rare
Bull L'Attache	1987	CS	Rare
Cambridge Z88	1988	A4	Plentiful
Casio FP200	1982	A4	Rare
Compaq Lte	1987	CS	Rare
Commodore LCD	1985	CS	Rare
Convergent Workslate	1983	A4	Rare
Data General 1	1983	CS	Rare

Data General 1 Model 2	1984	CS	Scarce
Datavue Snap	1987	CS	Rare
Datavue Spark	1988	CS	Scarce
Dell 316LT	1990	CS	Rare
Dulmont Magnum	1983	CS	Rare
Epson HX 20	1981	A4	Plentiful
Epson PX-4	1984	CS	Rare
Epson PX-8	1984	CS	Common
Epson PX-16	1988	CS	Rare
Epson Equity LT	1988	CS	Common
Epson Q150A	1989	CS	Rare
Fujitsu FM 18 Pi	1985	CS	Rare
Gateway 2000 Handbook	1993	CS	Rare
Gavilan	1983	CS	Rare
Grid Compass 1101	1982	CS	Rare
Grid Gridcase 3	1986	CS	Scarce
Grid 1520	1986	CS	Common
Grid lite 1032	1987	CS	Rare
Grid 140 XT	1988	CS	Rare
Hewlett Packard 110	1984	CS	Common
Hyundai Super LT3	1989	CS	Rare
IBM 5140	1987	CS	Plentiful

IBM PC Radio	198?	CS	Rare
KayPro 2000	1985	CS	Scarce
Kyotronic 85	1983	A4	Common
Laser PC4	1983	A4	Plentiful
MicroOffice Roadrunner	1984	A4	Rare
*NEC 8201A	1983	A4	Plentiful
NEC 8401A	1984	CS	Scarce
NEC 8500	1984	A4	Rare
NEC Multispeed EL-2	1988	CS	Common
NEC Multispeed HD	1987	CS	Rare
NEC Ultralite	1988	CS	Scarce
Olivetti M-10	!983	A4	Common
Olivetti M-15	1987	CS	Rare
Panasonic CF-150	1989	CS	Scarce
Panasonic CF-170	1989	CS	Scarce
Psion MC-200	1989	CS	Rare
Psion MC-400	1989	CS	Rare
Sanyo LT-16	1988	CS	Rare
Sharp 5000	1983	CS	Rare
Sharp PC-2500	1984	A4	Rare
Sharp PC4501	1987	CS	Rare
Sharp PC4600	1988	CS	Rare

Sharp P-5500	1988	CS	Rare
Sharp MZ100	1989	CS	Rare
Sony SMC210DL6	1985	CS	Rare
Sord 1S 11	1983	A4	Rare
Sord IS11C	1985?	CS	Rare
Tandy TRS-100	1983	A4	Plentiful
Tandy TRS 80 200	1985	CS	Common
Tandy 600	1985	CS	Common
Tandy 1100FD	1986	CS	Common
Tandy 1400 LT	1987	CS	Common
Tava Truimph	198?	CS	Rare
Teleram T-3000	1984	A4	Rare
TI LT220	1988	CS	Rare
TI "Pro Lite"	1985	CS	Rare
Toshiba T-3100	1986	CS	Common
Toshiba T-1000	1987	CS	Plentiful
Toshiba T-1000SE	1988	CS	Scarce
Toshiba T-1100 Plus	1987	CS	Common
Toshiba T1200XE	1987	CS	Scarce
Toshiba T-3200	1989	CS	Scarce
Tulip LT 286	1989	CS	Rare
Visual Technology	1983	CS	Scarce

Wang WLTC	1986	CS	Rare
Xerox Sunrise 1800	1983	A4	Rare
Zenith ZFL-181-93	1987	CS	Plentiful
Zenith ZWL-183-92	1987	CS	Common
Zenith 184-2	1987	CS	Scarce
Zenith Z-150	1988	CS	Rare
Zenith Minisport	1989	CS	Scarce

Vintage Laptop Computers

Amstrad PPC640

This is a very unusual computer and it is what I call a crossover between a laptop and a portable. The PPC640's appearance was one of a kind and nothing like it has been made again. It was known for its very poor display.

Rarity Scale: Common

MANUFACTURER:	Amstrad	TEXT MODES:	25 Line x 40 Character
ORGIN:	US	GRAPHIC MODE:	640x200
YEAR:	1988	SIZE:	19.5x9.0x4.1"
CPU:	80C86 or V-30	WEIGHT:	12.0#
SPEED:	4.77 or 8.0Mhz	KEYBOARD:	102 Keys
RAM:	640K	POWER SUPPLY:	AC Adapter w/battery
ROM:	16K	PRICE:	App 1700 DM
DISPLAY:	Green LCD	UNUSUAL FEATURES:	Unusual Appearance

APPLE POWERBOOK 100

The Powerbook 100 was Apple's first true small laptop computer. It was cute but missing a lot of required features. It was to be used by people on a budget. The 100 did not sell well due to its cost ($2500) as many felt the features, or lack of, didn't justify its high price. The Macintosh Portable was thought by some to be Apple's first laptop but it was a very big and heavy computer. I understand the 100 was patterned after the Macintosh Portable, but in a laptop format.

Rarity Scale: Scarce

MANUFACTURER:	Apple	TEXT MODES:	25 Line x 80 Character
ORGIN:	US	GRAPHIC MODES:	640 x 400
YEAR:	1991	SIZE:	8.5x11.0x1.6"
CPU:	6800	WEIGHT:	5.2#
SPEED:	16.0MHZ	KEYBOARD:	63 Key
RAM:	2Megs	POWER SUPPLY:	AC Adapter w/battery
ROM:	256K	PRICE:	$2500.00 (List)
DISPLAY:	Mono LCD	UNUSUAL FEATURES:	Trackball Mouse

Bondwell Pro 8 T

The Bondwell XT 80C88 was a relatively low powered laptop made in Hong Kong for American sales. It came with a modem, parallel, serial, and CRT ports, plus an external FDD. This model featured a hard drive which was unusual for this era's laptops. It was not a popular machine resulting in very few being sold. The Pro 8 T is a very difficult laptop to locate.

Rarity scale: Rare

MANUFACTURER:	Bondwell Industries	TEXT MODES:	16 Line x 80 Character
ORGIN:	UK	GRAPHIC MODE:	640 x 200
YEAR:	1985	SIZE:	12.0x13.5x3.5"
CPU:	8088	WEIGHT:	12.5
SPEED:	8.0MHZ	KEYBOARD:	92 Keys
RAM:	640K	POWER SUPPLY:	AC Adapter w/battery
ROM:	Unk	PRICE:	$1295.00
DISPLAY:	Mono LCD	UNUSUAL FEATURES:	None

Bondwell 200A

The Bondwell 200 was another laptop from the now defunct Bondwell Industries. For its time, it was a very beautiful laptop with a very slow 80C86 CPU and 128K of RAM which was upgradeable. A SD floppy drive was featured as was a large 10.5" supertwist LCD display. The 200A ran MS DOS. In Germany this laptop sold as the Highscreen B 200.

Rarity Scale: Scarce

MANUFACTURER: Bondwell Industries		TEXT MODE	16 Line x 80 Character
ORGIN:	UK	GRAPHIC MODE:	640 x 400
YEAR:	1988	SIZE:	12.0x12.5x2.5#
CPU:	80C88	WEIGHT:	6.5#
SPEED:	8.0MHZ	KEYBOARD:	8l Keys
RAM:	128K	POWER SUPPLY:	AC Adapter w/battery
ROM:	Unk	PRICE:	Unk
DISPLAY:	Supertwist LCD	UNUSUAL FEATURES:	None

BULL HONEYWELL SX-L

The SX-L is an offspring of Bull's acquisition of Zenith Data Systems in the late 1980s, and was released at the tail end of 1989. This is an attractive laptop with Zenith characteristics.

Rarity Scale: Rare

MANUFACTURER:	Bull Corporation	TEXT MODES:	25 Line x 80 Character
ORGIN	US:	GRAPHIC MODES:	640 x 400
YEAR:	1989	SIZE:	12.0x12.0x3.0"
CPU:	80286	WEIGHT:	12.0#
SPEED:	10.0MHZ (est)	KEYBOARD:	79 Keys
RAM:	640K	POWER SUPPLY:	AC Adapter w/battery
ROM:	Unk	PRICE:	Unk
DISPLAY:	Mono LCD	UNUSUAL FEATURES:	None

Cambridge Z-88

Armstrad bought the rights earlier to use the Sinclair name. Sir Clive Sinclair kept ownership of Sinclair Research but couldn't use the name. He then started a new company called Cambridge Research and the fruit of this endeavor was the Cambridge Z-88. This small laptop was fairly powerful with a Z80 CPU and featured a memory manager. Also, 32K Ram and 12K RAM cartridges were an option. The ROM contains a lot of software, including spreadsheet, word processor, and a database. This laptop lacks one much needed feature. It does not have an editor, or de-bugger, so mistakes resulted in the whole line having to be retyped.

Rarity scale: Plentiful

MANUFACTURER:	Cambridge Res.	TEXT MODES:	8 Line x 106 Character
ORGIN:	Scotland	GRAPHIC MODES:	640 x 64
YEAR	1988:	SIZE:	8.2x11.5x1.0"
CPU:	Z80	WEIGHT:	3.2#
SPEED:	3.28MHZ	KEYBOARD:	1 piece Molded 54 Key
RAM:	32K	POWER SUPPLY:	AC Adapter or Battery
ROM:	128K	PRICE:	Unk
DISPLAY:	Mono LCD	UNUSUAL FEATURES:	Molded Keyboard

Casio FP200

Casio is a very successful manufacturer of calculators and watches. Their first ventures into computers had failed, but with the FP 200 they took a different path and were able to carve out a niche in the market place. This is basically a spreadsheet machine and uses built in software called CELT (Casio Easy Language Table). It is built around the CMOS version of the Z80 CPU, with 8K of RAM. The FP200 requires a recorder, cassette tape, or single sided floppy disc for data storage. It has a full size keyboard and output ports are provided for a parallel printer with an RS232 serial device for other items.

Rarity Scale: Rare

MANUFACTURER:	Casio	TEXT MODES:	8 Line x 20 Character
ORGIN:	US	GRAPHIC MODE:	140 x 64
YEAR:	1982	SIZE:	8.7x12.2x2.2"
CPU:	Z80	WEIGHT:	3.4#
SPEED:	4.0MHZ	KEYBOARD:	70 Key
RAM:	8K	POWER SUPPLY:	AC Adapter or Batteries
ROM:	32K	PRICE:	$499.00
DISPLAY:	Mono LCD	UNUSUAL FEATURES:	None

Compaq LTE

The LTE was Compaq's first venture into the laptop business. It was built around the 80C86 CPU and runs DOS applications. This unit features a 21 Meg hard drive, a built in floppy disk drive and modem. This is a rare laptop as very few have survived.

Rarity Scale: Rare

MANUFACTURER:	Compaq Corp	TEXT MODES:	25 Line x 80 Character
ORGIN:	US	GRAPHIC MODES:	640 x 480
YEAR:	1989	SIZE:	8.5x11.0x2.0"
CPU:	80C86	WEIGHT:	7.0#
SPEED:	10.0MHZ	POWER SUPPLY:	AC Adapter w/battery
RAM:	6Meg	KEYBOARD:	80 Key
ROM:	Unk	PRICE:	Unk
DISPLAY:	Mono LCD	UNUSUAL FEATURES:	None

Convergent Technologies "Workslate"

Convergent Technologies of Santa Rosa, CA. released the "Workslate" at the same time as the Tandy Model 100. It was built to be used primiarly as a spread-sheet machine. I consider this unit to be a crossover between a laptop and a handheld computer. The keyboard with circular rubber keys, made text hard to type. The "Workslate" had a tape drive to record or play data, a 300 baud modem, and a printer port. It was first available in an American Express Christmas catalog slated to be sold as a novelty item. 200,000 units were forecast to be sold per year but only 5,000 were purchased in the US, and a couple hundred more in Europe. This forced production to cease in 1984 and the company reportedly lost over $15 million.

Rarity Scale: Plentiful

MANUFACTURER:	Convergent Tech	TEXT MODES:	16 Line x 46 Character
ORGIN:	US	GRAPHIC MODES:	Unk
YEAR:	1983	SIZE:	8.5x11.0x1.0"
CPU:	6303	WEIGHT:	2.3#
SPEED:	1.228MHZ	KEYBOARD:	66 Keys
RAM:	16K	POWER SUPPLY:	Adapter or Batteries
ROM:	64K	PRICE:	$895.00
DISPLAY:	Mono LCD	UNUSUAL FEATURES:	Rubber Keyboard

DataVue "Snap1+1"

The DataVue "Snap 1+1" was 1 of 2 laptop computers manufactured by the company. The unusual thing about this laptop was its orange display. The "Snap" had very little success in the laptop market due to its high price and extremely tough market competition. DataVue went out of business in 1993. This is a scarce laptop, very few have surfaced.

Rarity Scale: Rare

MANUFACTURER:	DataVue Corp	TEXT MODES:	16 Line x 80 Character
ORGIN:	US	GRAPHIC MODE:	640 x 200
YEAR:	1987	SIZE:	13.0x13.0x3.0"
CPU:	8088	WEIGHT:	12.0#
SPEED:	4.77MHZ	KEYBOARD:	83 Keys
RAM:	640K	POWER SUPPLY:	AC Adapter w/battery
ROM:	Unk	PRICE:	$2395.00
DISPLAY	Orange Plasma:	UNUSUAL FEATURES:	Orange Display

DataVue "Spark"

The DataVue "Spark" laptop was considered by some to be one of the prettiest laptops ever built. The "Spark" had an Intel 80C88 CPU and featured a blue display built by Epson which could support 16 colors. DOS was the operating system used on this laptop but it needed a boot disc to do anything. Very few "Sparks" were ever sold. The DataVue Corporation folded in 1993.

Rarity Scale: Scarce

MANUFACTURER:	DataVue Corp	TEXT MODES:	25 Line x 80 Character
ORGIN:	US	GRAPHIC MODES:	320 x 200
YEAR:	1987	SIZE:	12.8x13.0x2.3"
CPU:	8088—V20/30	WEIGHT:	9.5#
SPEED:	9.77MHZ	KEYBOARD:	76 Key IBM Style
RAM:	640K	POWER SUPPLY:	AC Adapter w/battery
ROM:	384K	PRICE:	$1195.00
DISPLAY:	Blue LCD	UNUSUAL FEATURES:	Blue Display

Data General One Model 2

The Data General One turned out to be one of the first MS DOS laptops to hit the market. It is built around the 80C88 CPU,and had some nice built in software. The Model 2 had double serial ports but they were not PC compatible. This laptop was equipped with two 3½ floppy disc drives, a nice feature that was ahead of its time. This machine was not overly successful in the market place. The DG1 was not a heavy computer and overall, it was a pretty nice design.

Rarity Scale: Scarce

MANUFACTURER:	Data General	TEXT MODES:	25 Line x 80 Character
ORGIN:	US	GRAPHIC MODE:	640 x 256
YEAR:	1984	SIZE:	11.3x13.5x3.0"
CPU:	8088	WEIGHT:	14.2#
SPEED:	4.0MHZ	KEYBOARD:	79 Keys
RAM:	256K	POWER SUPPLY:	AC Adaptor w/battery
ROM:	32K	PRICE:	$2895.00
DISPLAY:	Mono LCD	UNUSUAL FEATURES:	None

Dell 316 LT

The Dell 316 LT was the company's first venture into the laptop business. This unit included the new 80386 CPU and came equipped with either 20 or 40 Meg hard drive. Very few of these survived and locating one can be   extremely difficult.

:

Rarity Scale: Rare

MANUFACTURER:	Dell Corp	TEXT MODES:	25 Line x 80 character
ORGIN:	US	GRAPHIC MODE:	640 x 400
YEAR:	1990	SIZE:	12.7x14.2x3.3
CPU:	80386	WEIGHT:	13.0#
SPEED:	6.0MHZ	KEYBOARD:	83 Keys
RAM:	640K	POWER SUPPLY:	AC Adapter w/battery
ROM:	Unk	PRICE:	$3300.00
DISPLAY:	Blue LCD/CGA	UNUSUAL FEATURES:	Blue Display

Dulmont "Magnum"

The Dulmont "Magnum" was the company's first computer and was built in Australia. The "Magnum" was called "Kookaburra" on foreign markets. The unit is PC compatible, and contains a rechargeable Ni-Cad battery, which gave up to 10-12 hours of use. It was considered to be one of the first full function laptops manufactured. The "Magnum" was released in France in June, of 1984. This is a desirable and sought after laptop, locating one is extremely difficult.

Rarity Scale: Rare

MANUFACTURER:	Dulmont	TEXT MODES:	8 Line x 80 Character
ORGIN:	Australia	GRAPHIC MODES:	Unk
YEAR:	1984	SIZE:	12.2x10.7x2.3"
CPU:	80186	WEIGHT:	10.5#
SPEED:	8.0MHZ	KEYBOARD:	76 Keys
RAM:	96K	POWER SUPPLY:	AC Adapter w/battery
ROM:	128K	PRICE:	$3995.00
DISPLAY:	Mono LCD	UNUSUAL FEATURES:	None

Epson HX-20

The HX-20 is considered by some to be the first true laptop computer. It contains a small built-in printer which can print text or graphics, There is a small cassette tape recorder onboard which was considered fast for its day. The recorder could be removed and replaced with a ROM cartridge. The HX-20 featured a Zilog Z80 CPU which made it a fairly quick laptop. This was one of the "A4" machines.

Rarity Scale: Plentiful

MANUFACTURER:	Epson Corporation	TEXT MODES:	4 Line x 20 Character
ORGIN:	Japan/US	GRAPHIC MODES:	120 x 32
YEAR:	1982	SIZE:	8.5x11.5x2.0"
CPU:	Zilog Z80	WEIGHT:	3.0#
SPEED:	0.7MHZ	KEYBOARD:	68 Keys
RAM:	16K	POWER SUPPLY:	AC Adaptor
ROM:	32K	PRICE:	$599.00
DISPLAY:	Mono LCD	UNUSUAL FEATURES:	1st A4 Style Laptop

Epson PX-4

The PX-4 was a successor to the HX-20. The main difference was an adjustable display to change the angle which improved viewing. On the right side of the machine was a port to attach a tape recorder. Other peripherals were available for this laptop.

Rarity Scale: Rare

MANUFACTURER:	Epson Corporation	TEXT MODES:	8 Line x 40 Character
ORGIN:	Japan/US	GRAPHIC MODES:	240 x 64
YEAR:	1984	SIZE:	8.5x11.0x2.0"
CPU:	Z80	WEIGHT:	3.5#
SPEED:	3.7MHZ	KEYBOARD:	72 Keys
RAM:	64K	POWER SUPPLY:	AC Adaptor w/battery
ROM:	96K	PRICE:	$899.00
DISPLAY:	Mono LCD	UNUSUAL FEATURES:	None

Epson PX-8 "Geneva"

The PX-8 was a successor to the PX-4, and HX-20, and included a larger display as its main improvement. Software included a word processor and spread sheet. Dual 5.25" floppy drives were available, as was a stand alone 3.5" floppy disc drive. The PX-8 was designed to work with CP/M programs but it needed modifications due to the display system. This unit was sold in Japan as the Epson HC-88.

Rarity Scale: Plentiful

MANUFACTURER:	Epson Corporation	TEXT MODES:	8 Line x 80 Character
ORGIN:	Japan/US	GRAPHIC MODE:	480 x 64
YEAR:	1984	SIZE:	8.5x11.5x3.0"
CPU:	Zilog Z80	WEIGHT:	6.2#
SPEED:	2.45MHZ	KEYBOARD:	72 Keys
RAM:	16K	POWER SUPPLY:	AC Adapter w/battery
ROM:	32K	PRICE:	$995.00
DISPLAY:	Mono LCD	UNUSUAL FEATURES	Very Colorful Laptop

Epson Equity LT

The Equity LT was the 1st full sized "laptop" manufactured by Epson. It featured two floppy disc drives, one on each side of the laptop. Since the battery could not be removed for recharging a power source had to be near by. Only 2 parallel ports were available, one was for the external disk drive, the other had to be shared by the printer and other peripherals.

Rarity Scale: Common

MANUFACTURER:	Epson Corp	TEXT MODE:	25 Line x 80 Character
ORGIN:	Japan/US	GRAPHIC MODE:	640 x 200
YEAR:	1988	KEYBOARD:	85 Keys
CPU:	8088 or V30	SIZE:	12.2x13.6x3.1"
SPEED:	4.77Mhz	WEIGHT:	12.6#
RAM:	640K	POWER SUPPLY:	AC Adapter/Battery
ROM:	16K	PRICE:	$2847.00
DISPLAY:	Supertwist LCD	UNUSUAL FEATURES:	None

Ericsson

The Ericsson was a hunk of a laptop. It was one of the crossovers between a laptop and a portable computer. It had laptop characteristics, but the bulk of a portable. It had a couple of interesting features-one was the detachable keyboard and the other a red/orange display. This was indeed a very unusual computer.

Rarity Scale: Rare

MANUFACTURER:	Ericsson	TEXT MODES:	25 Line x 80 Character
ORGIN:	Japan/Sweden	GRAPHIC MODES:	640 x 400
YEAR:	1985	SIZE:	12.6x15.6x4.5"
CPU:	8088	WEIGHT:	16.5#
SPEED:	8.0MHZ	KEYBOARD:	84 Keys
RAM:	256K	POWER SUPPLY:	Power Plug
ROM:	16K	PRICE:	$2995.00
DISPLAY:	Red/Orange Plasma	UNUSUAL FEATURES:	Detachable Keyboard

Gateway 2000 "Handbook"

This was Gateway's first attempt into the laptop market. At the time it was the smallest laptop manufactured which was considered to be full function. The 2000 also featured a full keyboard, a 20 Meg hard drive, also available was a 3.5" floppy disc drive. This was a real cute little laptop.

Rarity Scale: Rare

MANUFACTURER:	Gateway	TEXT MODES:	16 Line x 80 Character
ORGIN:	US	GRAPHIC MODE :	640 x 200
YEAR:	1993	SIZE:	6.0x10.0x1.3"
CPU:	80186	WEIGHT:	2.7#
SPEED:	6.0MHZ	KEYBOARD:	78 Keys
RAM:	640K	POWER SUPPLY:	AC Adapter, AA Batteries
ROM:	Unk	PRICE:	Unk
DISPLAY:	Blue LCD	UNUSUAL FEATURES	Small and Blue Display

Gavilan

The Gavilan was a very innovative laptop with many features. It had a touch mouse pad on the keyboard and ran two operating systems, GOS and DOS. Problems plagued the company from the start, a shortage of operating capital and not being able keep up with production of this desirable laptop. There was also stiff competition, and the computer was not PC compatible. These problems doomed the Gavilan-the company closed after 2 years of production. Manny Fernandez lost $2 million trying to keep his dream alive. Today, the Gavilan is very rare and hard to find.

Rarity Scale: Rare

MANUFACTURER:	Gavilan	TEXT MODE:	8 Line x 66 Character
ORGIN:	US	GRAPHIC MODE:	644 x 566
YEAR:	1983	KEYBOARD:	68 Keys
CPU:	8088	SIZE:	11.4x11.4x2.7"
SPEED:	5Mhz	WEIGHT:	9.4#
RAM:	32K	POWER SUPPLY:	AC Adaptor w/battery
ROM:	48K	PRICE:	$3995.00- Printer $1.000
DISPLAY:	Mono LCD	UNUSUAL FEATURES:	Touch Pad Mouse

Grid Compass 1101

The Grid Compass 1101 is the highlight of my collection because of its connection to space shuttle history. It is a very rare laptop, very few have surfaced. It featured bubble memory (a very expensive item) used only in a few laptops and a gas plasma display, which was also used very sparingly on laptops. An external disk drive was also an available option. The 1101s were covered in a black magnesium case making them very durable as were most Grid laptops. More next page:

Rarity Scale: Rare

MANUFACTURER:	Grid	TEXT MODES:	16 Line x ?? Character
ORGIN:	US	GRAPHIC MODES:	320 x 240
YEAR:	1982	SIZE:	11.8x14.5x3.0"
CPU:	8086	WEIGHT:	10.7#
SPEED:	4.77MHZ	KEYBOARD:	Querty 57 Key
RAM:	128K	POWER SUPPLY:	AC Adapter
ROM:	512K	PRICE:	$8000-9000.00
DISPLAY:	Gas Plasma	UNUSUAL FEATURES:	First Clamshell Laptop

The Grid Compass 1101 was the first laptop produced by Grid and was supposedly designed by/for NASA for use on the first space shuttle (Columbia) in 1982. They were reportedly used onboard to plot the flight of the shuttle's position in relation to the earth, along with other tasks. It is said a photo exists of an 1101 floating about the cabin during a space mission. I cannot verify this as I have not found the photo. I did discover photos from a NASA photo gallery showing what I believe to be a Compass 1101 being used on two missions, (STS-051) in June 1985, and (ST-067). I have looked at photos of what I believe to be the "Gridcase" series, and the Grid 1520/30 series being used as late as 1990, but I cannot prove whether these prints were during an actual mission or training missions. These prints are available to view on the NASA website, if you have the patience and time (which I had) to go through thousands of photos to find them. It is unknown how long or how many of the 1101s were used on space mission programs.

The Grid 1101 was a very expensive laptop, besides being used by NASA, it was used by the military and as someone elegantly put it, and I quote, "a few others with deep pockets and a perceived need". You can see why the 1101 is such a sought after laptop due to its connection with the doomed space shuttle "Columbia".

Incidentally, another interesting fact I found during my research, Velcro was invented by NASA to fasten laptops and other small items to tables, consoles, and bulkheads, to keep them from floating around the cabin during space flight.

This information contains my beliefs based on printed material gleaned from many years of research.

Gridcase 3 Plus

The Gridcase 3 was one in a long line of Grid laptops that were used on space shuttle missions. The Gridcase 3 like most Grid laptops was built into a magnesium-alloy case and was considered almost indestructible.

Rarity Scale: Scarce

MANUFACTURER:	Grid	TEXT MODES:	25 Line x 80 Character
ORGIN:	US	GRAPHIC MODE:	640 x 400
YEAR:	1986	SIZE:	11.0x15.0x2.0:
CPU:	8088	WEIGHT:	12.0#
SPEED:	4.77MHZ	KEYBOARD:	71 Keys
RAM:	512K	POWER SUPPLY:	AC Adapter
ROM:	Unk	PRICE:	Unk
DISPLAY:	Mono LCD	UNUSUAL FEATURES:	Metal Case

Grid 1520

This looked much like the Gridcase 3 and was one of the first laptops along with the Toshiba 3100 to feature the 80286 CPU chip. It was another of the almost indestructible laptops made by Grid. It is my understanding the 1520/30 was also used by NASA on space shuttles.

Rarity Scale: Common

MANUFACTURER:	Grid	TEXT MODES:	25 Line x 80 Character
ORGIN:	US	GRAPHIC MODES:	640 x 200
YEAR:	1986	SIZE:	15.0x11.5x2.5"
CPU:	80286	WEIGHT:	12.0#
SPEED:	Unk	KEYBOARD:	72 Keys
RAM:	640K	POWER SUPPLY:	Power Cord
ROM:	Unk	PRICE:	Unk
DISPLAY:	Mono LCD	UNUSUAL FEATURES:	None

Gridlite 1032

This version of Grid computer is less novel than earlier models. One of the strong features of this laptop is its blue/yellow super twist display which can be viewed at an angle. This laptop runs DOS.

Rarity Scale: Rare

MANUFACTURER:	Grid	TEXT MODES:	25 Line x 80 Character
ORGIN:	US	GRAPHIC MODES:	320 x 640
YEAR:	1987	SIZE:	11.3x13.3x3.0"
CPU:	8086	WEIGHT:	8.5
SPEED:	14.77MHZ	KEYBOARD:	71 Keys
RAM:	128K	POWER SUPPLY:	AC Adapter
ROM:	1M	PRICE:	$1750.00
DISPLAY:	Blue/Yellow	UNUSUAL FEATURES:	Color Display

Grid 140 XT

The Grid 140 XT was based on the Tandy 1400FD. It had a 2400 baud modem and ran MS DOS. No other information is available. Another of the very scarce laptops manufactured by Grid.

Rarity Scale: Rare

MANUFACTURER:	Grid Corporation	TEXT MODES:	16 Line x 80 Character
ORGIN:	US	GRAPHIC MODE:	640 x 200
YEAR:	1988	SIZE:	12.0x14.0x3.0
CPU:	8086, NEC V20	WEIGHT:	12.2#
SPEED:	8.0MHZ	POWER SUPPLY:	AC Adapter w/battery
RAM:	640K	KEYBOARD	76 Key
ROM:	Unk	PRICE:	Unk
DISPLAY	Blue LCD:	UNUSUAL FEATURES:	Blue Display

Hewlett Packard HP-110

It was extremely good timing for HP to introduce a laptop computer while IBM and Apple were not yet in the laptop market. The 110 was somewhat compatible with its big brother, the HP-150. For much better viewing the display could be adjusted to any angle.

Rarity Scale: Plentiful

MANUFACTURER:	Hewlett-Packard	TEXT MODES:	16 Line x 80 Character
ORGIN:	US	GRAPHIC MODES:	480 x 128
YEAR:	1984	SIZE:	10.0x13.0x3.0"
CPU:	8086	WEIGHT:	9.2#
SPEED:	5.33MHZ	KEYBOARD:	Querty 83 Key
RAM:	256K	POWER SUPPLY:	AC Adapter w/battery
ROM:	384K	PRICE:	$2995.00
DISPLAY:	Mono LCD	UNUSUAL FEATURES:	None

Hyundai Super LT-3

Nothing much is known about this obscure laptop except the specs below. This is a very rare laptop. Wouldn't it be interesting if this was built by the same company that builds autos??

Rarity Scale: Rare

MANUFACTURER:	Hyundai Corp	TEXT MODES:	16 Line x 80 Character
ORGIN:	Korea/US	GRAPHIC MODE:	640 x 200
YEAR:	1989	SIZE:	12.5x13.0x3.0"
CPU:	80286	WEIGHT:	16.0#
SPEED:	Unk	KEYBOARD:	75 Keys
RAM:	1M	POWER SUPPLY:	AC Adapter w/battery
ROM:	Unk	PRICE:	Unk
DISPLAY:	Mono LCD	UNUSUAL FEATURES:	None

IBM 5140 Convertible

The 5140 was IBM's first attempt at manufacturing a "laptop" computer. It was a fairly advanced machine for IBM but was not up to the standards of its competition. This was their first use of surface mounted devices. It featured dual 3.5" floppy drives and a built in printer.

Rarity scale: Plentiful

MANUFACTURER:	IBM Corporation	TEXT MODES:	16 Line x 80 Character
ORGIN:	US	GRAPHIC MODES:	640 x 200
YEAR:	1986	SIZE:	18.5x12.0x3.0"
CPU:	8088	WEIGHT:	12.7#
SPEED:	4.77MHZ	KEYBOARD:	78 Keys
RAM	256K	POWER SUPPLY:	AC Adapter w/battery
ROM:	64K	PRICE:	$3495.00
DISPLAY:	Mono LCD	UNUSUAL FEATURES:	Built in Printer

IBM PC Radio

Very little is known about this laptop except it has a printer integrated into the unit.

Rarity Scale: Rare

MANUFACTURER:	IBM Corporation	TEXT MODES:	25 Line x 80 Character
ORGIN:	US	GRAPHIC MODE:	640 x 400
YEAR:	Unk	SIZE:	10.5x12.5x2.5 App
CPU:	80186	WEIGHT:	6.0#
SPEED:	5-10.0MHZ	KEYBOARD:	Query 79 Key
RAM:	640K	POWER SUPPLY:	Unk
ROM:	Unk	PRICE:	Unk
DISPLAY:	CGA Supertwist	UNUSUAL FEATURES:	None

Kaypro 2000

The Kaypro 2000 was a very futuristic looking laptop and used the NEC V20 CPU chip. The case is black brushed aluminum. The 2000 had a built-in modem and contained a rechargeable battery. This laptop had a very unique feature-it powered on/off by opening or closing the display.

Rarity Scale: Common

MANUFACTURER:	Kaypro Corp	TEXT MODES:	25 Line x 80 Character
ORGIN:	US	GRAPHIC MODE:	640 x 200
YEAR:	1985	SIZE:	13.2x11.5x2.8"
CPU:	NEC V20	WEIGHT:	12.1#
SPEED:	4.77MHZ	KEYBOARD:	77 Keys
RAM:	1256K	POWER SUPPLY:	AC Adapter w/battery
ROM:	Unk	PRICE:	$1995.00
DISPLAY:	Mono LCD	UNUSUAL FEATURES:	Darth Vader look.

Kyotronic 85

In the early 1980s Kyocera of Japan designed a great portable computer based on the Intel 80C85 CPU. The design was so innovative Tandy, Olivetti, and NEC licensed it from Kyocera. They in turn released their own version of the laptop with similar features. The 85 contained no data storage except a cassette recorder, or an optional external 5 ¼ floppy drive. The BASIC programming language was the last system in which most of the code was written by Bill Gates. The Kyotronic 85 was one of the first laptops manufactured.

Rarity Scale: Common

MANUFACTURER:	Kyocera	TEXT MODES:	8 Line x 40 Character
ORGIN:	Japan	GRAPHIC MODE:	240 x 64
YEAR:	1982	SIZE:	8.5x11.5x2.0"
CPU:	8085	WEIGHT:	3.8#
SPEED:	2.4MHZ	KEYBOARD:	Querty 56 Key
RAM:	16K	POWER SUPPLY	AA Batteries
ROM:	32K	PRICE:	$600.00
DISPLAY:	Mono LCD	UNUSUAL FEATURES:	Original Tandy Clone

Laser PC-4

To call this a laptop may be stretching it a bit. I consider it to be a cross-over between a laptop and a calculator?? Very little information is available on this unit.

Rarity Scale: Plentiful

MANUFACTURER:	Laser	TEXT MODES:	6 Line x 40 Character?
ORGIN:	US	GRAPHIC MODES:	Unk
YEAR:	1988	SIZE:	7.5x11.0x1.0"
CPU:	Unk	WEIGHT:	2.1#
SPEED:	Unk	KEYBOARD:	57 Keys
RAM:	Unk	POWER SUPPLY:	AA Batteries
ROM:	Unk	PRICE:	Unk
DISPLAY:	Mono LCD	UNUSUAL FEATURES:	None

NEC PC-8201A

This laptop was a spin-off of the Kyotronic 85 and was almost identical to the Tandy 100. It featured a different arrow key layout. A rechargeable battery pack was an available option. The PC-8201A was considered to be the most expandable of the Kyocera clones.

Rarity Scale: Plentiful

MANUFACTURER:	NEC Corporation	TEXT MODES:	8 Line x 40 Character
ORGIN:	Japan	GRAPHIC MODE:	240 x 64
YEAR:	1983	SIZE:	8.5x11.5x2.0"
CPU:	8085	WEIGHT:	3.4#
SPEED:	2.4MHZ	KEYBOARD:	Querty 56 Key
RAM:	32K	POWER SUPPLY:	AA Batteries
ROM:	32K	PRICE:	App $600.00
DISPLAY:	Mono LCD	UNUSUAL FEATURES:	None

NEC PC-8401A "Starlet"

The 8401A is a 2nd generation NEC laptop computer. It was the first of NEC's "clamshell" style laptops. The "Starlet" could be used with AA batteries or an optional AC adapter. It is larger and heavier than the 8201A and used the CP/M operation system. The unit came equipped with an optional floppy disc drive. The 8401A featured a power saving shutoff that turned the laptop off when not used within an allotted length of time.

Rarity scale: Scarce

MANUFACTURER:	NEC Corp	TEXT MODES:	6 Line x 80 Character
ORGIN:	Japan/US	GRAPHIC MODES:	480 x 128
YEAR:	1984	SIZE:	8.5x11.5x2.8"
CPU:	Zilog Z80	WEIGHT:	5.0#
SPEED:	4.0MHZ	KEYBOARD:	68 Keys
RAM:	64K	POWER SUPPLY:	AC Adaptor/battery
ROM:	96K	PRICE:	$995.00
DISPLAY:	Mono LCD	UNUSUAL FEATURES:	None

NEC Multispeed EL

The Multispeed EL featured a backlit display which was very easy to read. Like most backlit screens it gave off a slight hum. There were two floppy disc drives on the right side. This machine was not a small or lightweight laptop, as a matter of fact, it was pretty hefty. The keyboard was not the standard type or arrangement and had a separate numeric pad. There was no light onboard to indicate the battery was being charged.

Rarity Scale: Common

MANUFACTURER:	NEC Corp	TEXT MODE:	25 Line x 80 Character
ORGIN:	Japan/US	GRAPHIC MODES:	Unk
YEAR:	1988	KEYBOARD:	85 KEYS
CPU:	Zilog Z30	SIZE:	12.0x13.5x3.0"
SPEED:	4.77Mhz	WEIGHT:	12.2 #
RAM:	512K	POWER SUPPLY:	AC Adapter w/battery
ROM:	Unk	PRICE:	$2495.00
DISPLAY:	Backlit LCD	UNUSUAL FEATURES:	Backlit Display

NEC Multispeed HD

Nothing is known about this computer except the following specifications.

Rarity Scale: Rare

MANUFACTURER:	NEC Corporation	TEXT MODE:	25 Line x 60 Character
ORGIN:	Japan/US	GRAPHIC MODE:	Unk
YEAR:	1987	KEYBOARD:	85 Keys
CPU:	Unk	SIZE:	12.0x13.3x3.0"
SPEED:	12.0MHZ	WEIGHT:	12.2#
RAM:	640K	POWER SUPPLY:	AC Adapter/battery
ROM:	Unk	PRICE:	Unk
DISPLAY:	Backlit LCD	USUAL FEATURES:	None

NEC Ultralite 17-02

The Ultralite 17-02 had a 2 Meg hard drive while most units of the era had none. There was a 2400bps modem installed on the laptop. The 17-02 has an unusual blue screen. This NEC is a light weight computer, and a very attractive little laptop.

Rarity Scale: Scarce

MANUFACTURER:	NEC Corp	TEXT MODES:	25 Line x 80 Character
ORGIN:	Japan	GRAPHIC MODE:	640 x 200
YEAR:	1988	SIZE:	8.3x11.8x1.4"
CPU:	NEC V30	WEIGHT:	4.4#
SPEED:	8.14MHZ	KEYBOARD:	78 Keys
RAM:	640K	POWER SUPPLY:	AC Adapter w/battery
ROM:	2M	PRICE:	$2995.00
DISPLAY:	Blue LCD	UNUSUAL FEATURES:	Blue Display

Olivetti M-10

The M-10 is basically the same machine as the NEC 8201A and the Tandy 100, but with one major difference. The display can be adjusted for better viewing. Two of its nice features are, an excellent keyboard, and a large battery capacity. It was considered to be a very beautiful laptop by its owners and is a popular computer today with many new reporters.

Rarity Scale: Scarce

MANUFACTURER:	Olivetti	TEXT MODES:	8 Line x 40 Character
ORGIN:	Japan/Italy/US	GRAPHIC MODE:	240 x 64
YEAR:	1983	SIZE:	8.5x11.5x2.7
CPU:	80C85	WEIGHT:	5.0#
SPEED:	3.0MHZ	KEYBOARD:	Querty 68 Key
RAM:	32K	POWER SUPPLY:	AC Adaptor or batteries
ROM:	32K	PRICE:	App $1095.00
DISPLAY:	Mono LCD	UNUSUAL FEATURES:	None

Olivetti M-15

Little is known about this fairly obscure laptop. It was Olivetti's first and only "clamshell" laptop. The M-15 had an unusual feature-there were dials on the display board which gave it a different appearance. The M-15 ran DOS.

Rarity Scale: Rare

MANUFACTURER:	Olivetti	TEXT MODES:	25 Line x 80 Character
ORGIN:	Japan/Italy	GRAPHIC MODE:	640 x 200
YEAR:	1987	SIZE:	10.7x14.0x3.0
CPU:	8086	WEIGHT:	12.5#
SPEED:	4.77MHZ	KEYBOARD:	78 Keys
RAM:	512K	POWER SUPPLY:	AC Adapter w/battery
ROM:	16K	PRICE:	Unk
DISPLAY:	CGA LCD	UNUSUAL FEATURES:	Dials on Display Board

Panasonic BP 150

The Business Partner 150 was Panasonic's first laptop to be produced. It was IBM compatible and used a floppy disc for data storage. Overall, it was a nice, neat, compact little laptop, with an unusual green display.

Rarity Scale: Scarce

MANUFACTURER:	Matsushiba LTD	TEXT MODES:	25 Line x 80 Character
ORGIN:	Japan/US	GRAPHIC MODE:	640 x 200
YEAR:	1989	SIZE:	10.0x12.5x2.5"
CPU:	Zilog Z30,	WEIGHT:	6.5#
SPEED:	8.0MHZ	KEYBOARD:	84 Keys
RAM:	1M	POWER SUPPLY:	AC Adapter w/battery
ROM:	Unk	PRICE:	App $995.00
DISPLAY:	Green LCD	UNUSUAL FEATURES:	Green Display

Vintage Laptop Computers

Panasonic BP 170

The Panasonic BP 170 was the successor to the BP 150. There was not a lot of difference between the two except the color of the display. The BP 170 had a little faster CPU, but less RAM. This was also a neat laptop, but it is very difficult to locate.

Rarity Scale: Rare

MANUFACTURER:	Matsushita LTD.	TEXT MODES:	25 Line x 80 Character
ORGIN:	Japan/US	GRAPHIC MODE:	640 x 200
YEAR:	1989	SIZE:	10.0x12.0x2.0"
CPU:	8088	WEIGHT:	6.6#
SPEED:	8.0MHZ	KEYBOARD:	84 Keys
RAM:	640K	POWER SUPPLY:	AC Adapter w/battery
ROM:	Unk	PRICE:	App. $995.00
DISPLAY:	Blue LCD	UNUSUAL FEATURES:	Blue Display

Psion MC 400

The MC 400 was produced in the UK for European use along with the MC 200 and 600. These laptops were Psion's first attempt in the market. They were, and still are, basically a hand-held computer manufacturer. It was a high quality innovative little laptop. The Psion and the Gavilan were the only laptops of the era that offered a mouse, a very advanced feature. For some unknown reason the MC series did not fare well in the fast moving laptop market. I understand Psion later denied these were ever produced. This laptop is very rare.

Rarity Scale: Rare

MANUFACTURER:	Psion	TEXT MODES:	25 Line x 80 character
ORGIN:	UK	GRAPHIC MODE:	640 x 400
YEAR:	1989	SIZE:	10.2x12.1x2.1"
CPU:	8086	WEIGHT:	5.3#
SPEED:	3.8MHZ	KEYBOARD:	63 Keys
RAM:	640K	POWER SUPPLY:	AC Adapter or Batteries
ROM:	256K	PRICE:	695lbs (App$1995.00)
DISPLAY:	Mono LCD	UNUSUAL FEATURES:	Built-in Mouse Pad

Sanyo LT 16

Very little is known about this laptop except a few specs. It featured dual floppy disc drives for data storage. This is a very rare laptop, few have surfaced.

Rarity Scale: Rare

MANUFACTURER:	Sanyo	TEXT MODES:	16 Line x 80 Character
ORGIN:	Japan/US	GRAPHIC MODES:	640 x 200
YEAR:	1988	SIZE:	11.5x11.5x3.0"
CPU:	8088	WEIGHT:	7.0#
SPEED:	4.77MHZ	KEYBOARD:	76 Keys
RAM:	Unk	POWER SUPPLY:	AC Adapter w/battery
ROM:	16K	PRICE:	Unk
DISPLAY:	Mono LCD	UNUSUAL FEATURES:	None

Sharp PC-5000

This was the first of the Sharp laptops. The 5000 along with the Gavilan and the Grid Compass, were the first of the "clamshell" type laptops. It had an optional printer which connected to the back of the unit. The type of memory used (magnetic bubble) was very unusual. The Sharp 5000 ran DOS, but was not PC compatible. Software included a spreadsheet and a word processor.

Rarity Scale: Rare

MANUFACTURER:	Sharp Corp	TEXT MODES:	8 Line x 80 Character
ORGIN:	Japan/US	GRAPHIC MODES:	640 x 80
YEAR:	1983	SIZE:	12.8x12.0x
CPU:	8088	WEIGHT:	12.0#
SPEED:	4.77MHZ	KEYBOARD:	72 Keys
RAM:	128K	POWER SUPPLY:	AC Adapter
ROM:	192K	PRICE:	$1995.00
DISPLAY:	Mono LCD	UNUSUAL FEATURES:	Built in Printer

Sharp PC 4501

Little is known about this computer except the specs below. This was the 2nd laptop model manufactured by Sharp.

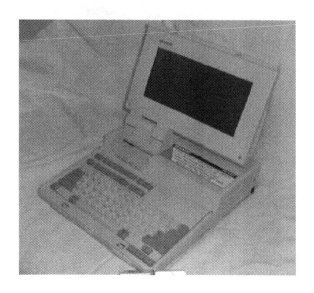

Rarity Scale: Rare

MANUFACTURER:	Sharp Corp	TEXT MODES:	16 Line x 80 Character
ORGIN:	Japan/US	GRAPHIC MODE:	Unk
YEAR:	1987	SIZE:	14.0x12.0x3.0"
CPU:	8086	WEIGHT:	10.7#
SPEED:	4.77MHZ	KEYBOARD:	78 Keys
RAM:	256K	POWER SUPPLY:	AC Adapter
ROM:	Unk	PRICE:	$1295.00
DISPLAY:	Supertwist LCD	UNUSUAL FEATURES:	None

Sharp PC 4600

Another in a line of obscure Sharp laptops. Little is known about it.

Rarity Scale: Rare

MANUFACTURER	Sharp Corp	TEXT MODES:	25 Line x 80 Character
ORGIN:	Japan/US	GRAPHIC MODE:	640 x 400
YEAR:	1987	SIZE:	13.5x12.0x3.0"
CPU:	8086	WEIGHT:	12.0#
SPEED:	4.77MHZ	KEYBOARD:	89 Keys
RAM:	640K	POWER SUPPLY:	AC Adapter
ROM:	Unk	PRICE:	Unk
DISPLAY:	Mono LCD	UNUSUAL FEATURES:	None

Sharp MZ-100

Like most other Sharp Computers, very little is known about this scarce laptop except the few specs below.

Rarity Scale: Rare

MANUFACTURER	Sharp Corp	TEXT MODES:	25 Line x 80 Character
ORGIN:	Japan/US	GRAPHIC MODE:	640 x 400
YEAR:	1989	SIZE:	12.0x13.5x3.0"
CPU:	NEC V30	WEIGHT:	12.0
SPEED:	10.0MHZ	KEYBOARD:	89 Keys
RAM:	640K	POWER SUPPLY:	AC Adapter w/battery
ROM:	Unk	PRICE:	Unk
DISPLAY:	Blacklit LCD	UNUSUAL FEATURES:	None

Sharp PC-5500

Very little is known about this laptop expect the following specifications. It does have a 40Meg hard drive. This is a big, big laptop.

Rarity Scale: Rare

MANUFACTURER:	Sharp Corp	TEXT MODES:	25 Line x 80 Character
ORGIN:	Japan/US	GRAPHIC MODE:	640 x 400
YEAR:	1988	SIZE:	12.0x17.0x3.0:
CPU:	80286	WEIGHT:	16.0# app.
SPEED:	10.0MHZ (est)	KEYBOARD:	79 Keys
RAM:	640K	POWER SUPPLY:	AC Adapter w/battery
ROM:	Unk	PRICE:	Unk
DISPLAY:	Mono VGA LCD	UNUSUAL FEATURES:	Built-in Printer

Vintage Laptop Computers

Sony M35

Information is limited on this laptop. It came with dual 3.5" floppy disc drives and a 300 baud modem. It operates on MS DOS 2.11. This laptop is rarely seen in the market place.

Rarity Scale: Rare

MANUFACTURER:	Sony Corp	TEXT MODES:	25 Line x 80 Character
ORGIN:	Japan	GRAPHIC MODE:	640 x 240
YEAR:	1985	SIZE:	14.0x11.5x3.0"
CPU:	8088	WEIGHT:	11.0#
SPEED:	4.77MHZ	KEYBOARD:	83 Keys
RAM:	640K	POWER SUPPLY:	Power Cord
ROM:	16K	PRICE:	Unk
DISPLAY:	Mono LCD	UNUSUAL FEATURES:	Built-in Printer

Tandy TRS-80 Model 100

This was the most famous and recognized vintage laptop computer ever produced. It was one of the Kyocera spin-offs that took the computer world by storm. At the time of its release the Model 100 was a sought after computer by newspapermen all over the globe. It is still used today by many reporters. I understand the Model 100's CPU was modified to be used on the rover, which was carried by NASA's Mars probe "Pathfinder", but I cannot verify this. The TRS-80 functioned on a version of BASIC.

Rarity Scale: Plentiful

MANUFACTURER:	Tandy Corp	TEXT MODES:	8 Line x 40 Character
ORGIN:	Japan/US	GRAPHIC MODE:	240 x 64
YEAR:	1983	SIZE:	8.5x11.5x2.0"
CPU:	8085	WEIGHT:	3.5#
SPEED:	3.0MHZ	KEYBOARD:	Querty 56 Key
RAM:	32K	POWER SUPPLY:	AA Batteries
ROM:	32K	PRICE:	$795.00
DISPLAY:	Mono LCD	UNUSUAL FEATURES:	None

Tandy Model 200

This laptop was basically the same as the Model 100 except it featured a larger "clamshell" type display. The model 200 contained more battery power, a popular addition.

Rarity Scale: Common

MANUFACTURER:	Tandy Corp	TEXT MODES:	16 Line x 40 Character
ORGIN:	Japan/US	GRAPHIC MODE:	240 x 128
YEAR:	1985	SIZE:	8.5x11.5x2.5"
CPU:	8085	WEIGHT:	3.0#
SPEED:	2.4MHZ	KEYBOARD:	Querty 56 K
RAM:	24K	POWER SUPPLY:	AA Batteries
ROM:	24K	PRICE:	$999.00
DISPLAY:	Mono LCD	UNUSUAL FEATURES:	None

Tandy Model 600

The Tandy model 600 laptop was much more powerful than the model 200. It had a larger display, a 300 baud modem, and expanded memory. This was a really nice laptop.

Rarity Scale: Common

MANUFACTURER:	Tandy Corporation	TEXT MODES:	16 Line x 80 Character
ORGIN:	Japan/US	GRAPHIC MODE:	480 x 128
YEAR:	1985	SIZE:	12.0x13.3x2.7"
CPU:	8088	WEIGHT:	9.5#
SPEED:	3.07MHZ	KEYBOARD:	72 Keys
RAM:	32K	POWER SUPPLY:	AC Adapter w/battery
ROM:	128K	PRICE:	$1599.00
DISPLAY:	Mono LCD	UNUSUAL FEATURES:	None

Tandy 1100 FD

The Tandy 1100FD laptop was not a brilliant move on Tandy's part. This machine was out classed by its competition before it was ever produced as others had faster CPU's and more features. It was an attractive laptop even though it was out dated.

Rarity Scale: Common

MANUFACTURER:	Tandy Corp	TEXT MODES:	25 Line x 80 Character
ORGIN:	Japan/US	GRAPHIC MODE:	640 x 200
YEAR:	1986	SIZE:	10.5x12.5x2.7"
CPU:	NEC V20	WEIGHT:	6.0#
SPEED:	10.0MHZ	KEYBOARD:	84 Keys
RAM:	640K	POWER SUPPLY:	AC adapter w/battery
ROM:	32K	PRICE:	Unk
DISPLAY:	Green LCD	UNUSUAL FEATURES:	Green Display

Tandy 1400LT

Tandy took a different approach when developing the 1400LT. It was a fairly heavy and bulky laptop, and was PC compatible. It had dual floppy disc drives, mounted on top of the keyboard. The 1400LT had a backlit display, which could be turned on and off. There was no light to indicate when the battery was being charged.

Rarity Scale: Common

MANUFACTURER:	Tandy Corp	TEXT MODE:	16 Line x 80 Character
ORGIN:	Japan/US	GRAPHIC MODE:	640 x 200
YEAR:	1987	SIZE:	14.5x12.5x3.0"
CPU:	8088	WEIGHT:	12.2#
SPEED:	7.16MHZ	KEYBOARD:	76 Keys
RAM:	768K	POWER SUPPLY:	AC adapter w/battery
ROM:	Unk	PRICE:	$1799.00
DISPLAY:	Backlit LCD	UNUSUAL FEATURES:	Backlit Display

Tava Triumph LT

This is a unit I consider a crossover between a laptop and portable. It had the laptop design, but was a big, big machine which was very heavy. It had dual 3.5" floppy disc drives for storing data. It featured a massive keyboard, and ran DOS. This is an obscure machine and very few have surfaced.

Rarity Scale: Rare

MANUFACTURER:	Tava USA	TEXT MODES:	16 Line x 80 Character
ORGIN:	Hong Kong/US	GRAPHIC MODE:	640 x 200
YEAR:	198?	SIZE:	18.0x12.5x3.0"
CPU:	80186	WEIGHT:	20.0#
SPEED:	Unk	KEYBOARD:	88 Keys
RAM:	640K	POWER SUPPLY:	Power Cord
ROM:	Unk	PRICE:	$2495.00
DISPLAY:	Mono LCD	UNUSUAL FEATURES:	BIG!!!

Texas Instruments LT-220

The TI-220 was one of two laptops produced by the company in the 1980s. It was a light, neat little machine. Very little information is available.

Rarity Scale: Rare

MANUFACTURER:	Texas Instrument	TEXT MODES:	25 Line x 80 Character
ORGIN:	US	GRAPHIC MODES:	Unk
YEAR:	1989	SIZE:	8.2x11.7x3.2
CPU:	8088	WEIGHT:	4.8#
SPEED:	Unk	KEYBOARD:	84 Keys
RAM: 128K	Unk	POWER SUPPLY:	AC Adapter w/battery
ROM:	Unk	PRICE:	Unk
DISPLAY:	Mono LCD	UNUSUAL FEATURES:	None

Toshiba T3100

This was the first laptop with an 80286 CPU and a hard drive. It was way ahead of its competition in these areas. The T3100 was very large and heavy which took some of the glamour away from its strong points.

Rarity Scale: Common

MANUFACTURER:	Toshiba America	TEXT MODES:	25 Line x 80 Character
ORGIN:	Japan/US	GRAPHIC MODES:	640 x 400
YEAR:	1986	SIZE:	12.2x14.2x3.1"
CPU:	80286	WEIGHT:	15.0#
SPEED:	10.0MHZ	KEYBOARD:	84 Keys
RAM:	1M	POWER SUPPLY	Power Cord:
ROM:	64K	PRICE:	$2987.00
DISPLAY:	Orange Plasma	UNUSUAL FEATURES:	Orange Plasma Display

Toshiba T1000

There are claims that the T1000 was the first real laptop. I consider this to be a questionable assumption since it was wasn't produced until 1987?? This was a very durable laptop and could take a beating and still function. It operated on DOS 2.11.

Rarity Scale: Plentiful

MANUFACTURER:	Toshiba America	TEXT MODES:	16 Line x 80 Character
ORGIN:	Japan/US	GRAPHIC MODE:	40 x 200
YEAR:	1987	SIZE:	11.5x12.0x2.0"
CPU:	8088	WEIGHT:	6.4#
SPEED:	4.77MHZ	KEYBOARD:	82 Keys
RAM:	512K	POWER SUPPLY:	AC Adapter w/ battery
ROM:	48K	PRICE:	$999.00
DISPLAY:	Mono LCD	UNUSUAL FEATURES:	None

Toshiba T1100 Plus

The T1100 Plus was logically the successor to the T1000. The 1100 came with dual 3.5" floppy disc drives and a rechargeable battery. The unit was capable of running up to a DOS 3.2 operating system.

Rarity Scale: Common

MANUFACTURER:	Toshiba America	TEXT MODES:	25 Line x 80 Character
ORGIN:	Japan/US	GRAPHIC MODE:	640 x 200
YEAR:	1987	SIZE:	11.5x12.0x2.7
CPU:	8088	WEIGHT:	9.9#
SPEED:	4.77MHZ	KEYBOARD:	81 Keys
RAM:	256K	POWER SUPPLY:	AC Adapter w/ battery
ROM:	32K	PRICE:	$1995.00
DISPLAY:	Mono LCD	UNUSUAL FEATURES:	None

Toshiba 1200XE

There were several varieties of T1200 Toshiba laptops, the FB, HB, and the XE. The 1200XE was one of a few laptops that were ahead of their time as they featured a powerful (for its era) 80286 CPU. Almost all others (except the Toshiba 3100, and Grid 1520) had slower CPU's in 1987 as did a few of the earlier 1200XE's.

Rarity Scale: Scarce

MANUFACTURER:	Toshiba America	TEXT MODES:	25 Line x 80 Character
ORGIN:	Japan/US	GRAPHIC MODE:	640 x 200
YEAR:	1987	SIZE:	11.0x12.0x2.0"
CPU:	8088/80286	WEIGHT:	8.5#
SPEED:	9.54MHZ	KEYBOARD:	82 Keys
RAM:	960K	POWER SUPPLY:	AC Adapter w/battery
ROM:	64K	PRICE:	$3495.00
DISPLAY:	Mono LCD	UNUSUAL FEATURES:	T-Carry Handle

Toshiba T1000SE

The T1000SE was an upgrade of the T-1000. A much nicer looking laptop but was not manufactured until 1989. By the time this machine was built, it was already outdated.

Rarity Scale: Rare

MANUFACTURER:	Toshiba America	TEXT MODE:	16 Line x 80 Character
ORGIN:	Japan/US	GRAPHIC MODE:	640 x 200
YEAR:	1989	KEYBOARD:	82 Keys
CPU:	8086	SIZE:	10.0x12.0x2.0"
SPEED:	4.77Mhz	WEIGHT:	6.4#
RAM:	Unk	POWER SUPPLY:	AC Adapter
ROM:	48K	PRICE:	Unk
DISPLAY:	Mono LCD	UNUSAL FEATURES:	Display

Toshiba T-3200

The T-3200 was an upgrade of the T3100 with faster CPU and more RAM, and a slightly different keyboard. In appearance this looked pretty much like the T-3100. Like many other computers built in the 1980's, I question why this model was produced?

Rarity Scale: Scarce

MANUFACTURER:	Toshiba America	TEXT MODES:	25 Line x 80 Character
ORGIN:	Japan/US	GRAPHIC MODES:	640 x 400
YEAR:	1989	SIZE:	14.0x15.0x4.0"
CPU:	80286	WEIGHT:	16.0#
SPEED:	12.0MHZ	KEYBOARD	85 Key
RAM:	1Meg	POWER SUPPLY:	AC Adapter /battery
ROM:	64K	PRICE:	$5299.00
DISPLAY:	Orange Plasma	UNUSUAL FEATURES:	Display

Tulip LT286

I have been able to decipher from some Dutch sites, this laptop was introduced in Feb 1989. A 20 or 40meg hard drive was installed. No more information is available except for the specs below.

Rarity Scale: Rare

MANUFACTURER:	Compudata Corp	TEXT MODES:	25 Line x 80 Character
ORGIN:	Netherlands	GRAPHIC MODES:	640 x 200
YEAR:	1989	SIZE:	12.7x13.3x3.2"
CPU:	80286	WEIGHT:	16.0#
SPEED:	12.0MHZ	KEYBOARD:	84 Key
RAM:	1M	POWER SUPPLY:	AC Adapter w/battery
ROM:	Unk	PRICE:	Unk
DISPLAY:	Mono LCD	UNUSUAL FEATURES:	None

Visual Commuter 1083

This huge computer is one I consider a crossover between the laptop and portable. The Commuter featured dual 5.25" floppy disc drives for data storage. This is all the information available except the following specs.

Rarity Scale: Scarce

MANUFACTURER:	Visual Tech	TEXT MODES:	8 Line x 80 Character
ORGIN:	US	GRAPHIC MODE:	640 x.200
YEAR:	1983	SIZE:	15.5x17.5x3.5"
CPU:	8086	WEIGHT:	22.0#
SPEED:	4.0MHZ	KEYBOARD:	83 Keys
RAM:	640K	POWER SUPPLY:	Power Cord
ROM:	32K ?	PRICE:	$1995.00
DISPLAY:	Mono LCD	UNUSUAL FEATURES:	Big & Heavy!!

Vintage Laptop Computers

Wang "WLTC"

The Wang "WLTC" is a very big laptop. It came with a built-in printer and a modem, for the traveler. A 10 Meg hard drive was an available option as were separate 5.25" floppy disc drives. The Wang ran DOS 3.2.

Rarity Scale: Rare

MANUFACTURER:	Wang Corporation	TEXT MODES:	16 Line x 80 Character
ORGIN:	US	GRAPHIC MODE:	640 x 400
YEAR:	1986	SIZE:	11.5x13.5x4.0"
CPU:	8086	WEIGHT:	16.0#
SPEED:	8.0MHZ	KEYBOARD:	87 Keys
RAM:	512K	POWER SUPPLY:	AC Adapter w/battery
ROM:	Unk	PRICE:	$3530.00
DISPLAY:	Mono LCD	UNUSUAL FEATURES:	Built-in Printer

Xerox "Sunrise" 1810

The Xerox "Sunrise" 1810 was produced in very small quantities. It had a CP/M system and a built-in 300 baud modem. There was also a micro tape recorder onboard for recording and playing data. This is one of the very earliest laptops.

Rarity Scale: Rare

MANUFACTURER:	Xerox Corporation	TEXT MODES:	3 Line x 80 Character
ORGIN:	US	GRAPHIC MODE:	Unk
YEAR:	1983	SIZE:	9.0x16.0x2.0"
CPU:	Zilog Z80	WEIGHT:	5.7#
SPEED:	4.0MHZ	KEYBOARD:	67 Keys
RAM:	64K	POWER SUPPLY:	AC Adapter
ROM:	32K	PRICE:	$2195.00
DISPLAY:	Mono LCD	UNUSUAL FEATURES:	Big, but not Heavy

Zenith ZFL 181-93

The ZFL 181-93 had dual pop-up 3.5" floppy disc drives for data storage. It had a large backlit display in a vivid blue color and 3 ports for attaching printers and other peripherals to the machine. The 181-93 featured a 1200 baud modem. This was one of many Zenith laptops of the era.

Rarity Scale: Plentiful

MANUFACTURER:	Zenith	TEXT MODES:	25 Line x 80 Character
ORGIN:	US	GRAPHIC MODE:	640 x 200
YEAR:	1987	SIZE:	11.5x15.5x3.0"
CPU:	8088	WEIGHT:	11.5#
SPEED:	4.77MHZ	KEYBOARD:	75 Keys
RAM:	640K	POWER SUPPLY:	AC Adapter w/battery
ROM:	Unk	PRICE:	$2395.00
DISPLAY:	Blue LCD	UNUSUAL FEATURES:	Blue Display

Zenith ZWL 183-92

Another of the many Zenith laptops produced in the 80s. All were pretty much alike.

Rarity Scale: Common

MANUFACTURER:	Zenith	TEXT MODES:	25 Line x 80 Character
ORGIN:	US	GRAPHIC MODE:	640 x 200
YEAR:	1987	SIZE:	13.0x15.0x3.5"
CPU:	8088	WEIGHT:	15.2#
SPEED:	4.77MHZ	KEYBOARD:	75 Keys
RAM:	640K	POWER SUPPLY:	AC Adapter w/battery
ROM:	Unk	PRICE:	Unk
DISPLAY:	Mono LCD	UNUSUAL FEATURES:	None

Zenith ZWL 184-02

The Zenith ZWL 184-02 "Supersport" laptop was another in a long line of Zenith computers. There were few internal changes, but externally, a smaller and lighter machine.

Rarity Scale: Scarce

MANUFACTURER:	Zenith	TEXT MODES:	25 Line x 80 Character
ORGIN:	US	GRAPHIC MODE:	640 x 200
YEAR:	1987	SIZE:	12.0x12.0x2.0"
CPU:	8088	WEIGHT:	10.0#
SPEED:	4.77MHZ	KEYBOARD:	74 Keys
RAM:	640K	POWER SUPPLY:	AC Adapter w/battery
ROM:	Unk	PRICE:	$2399.99
DISPLAY:	Mono LCD	UNUSUAL FEATURES	None

Zenith "Minisport"

Zenith finally produced something a little different! The "Minisport" was one of the first sub compact laptops. One of its unique features was the 2" double sided, double density, 720K floppy disc drive. This unit ran DOS. It was a very big improvement for Zenith.

Rarity Scale: Scarce

MANUFACTURER:	Zenith	TEXT MODES:	16 Line x 80 Character
ORGIN:	US	GRAPHIC MODE:	640 x 200
YEAR:	1989	SIZE:	12.5x9.7x1.3"
CPU:	8088	WEIGHT:	5.9#
SPEED:	4.77MHZ	KEYBOARD:	80 Keys
RAM:	1M	POWER SUPPLY:	AC Adapter w/ battery
ROM:	768K	PRICE:	$1999.00
DISPLAY:	Mono LCD	UNUSAL FEATURES:	Sub Compact

Vintage Laptop Computers

Other Known Laptops

The laptops listed on the following pages are units I've been unable to purchase but are known to exist. I've reached the point of being unable to find an additional major model more often than once or twice a year. A different manufacturer usually does not surface but once every couple of years. I have images of all except two of the listed models, but due to copyright laws, I am not permitted to reproduce them. Old-Computers.Com Museum has graciously permitted me to use images of their laptops that I do not have in my collection.

Ampere WS 1

This was a very unusual computer with an unusual design. It did not use the English language and contained numerous unique features. The WS1 did not pass the US FCC certification test so it was never sold in the US. The above along with its high price and small market makes it a very rare computer today.

No Image Available

Rarity Scale: Rare

MANUFACTURER:	Ampere	TEXT MODES	25 Line x 80 Character
ORGIN:	Japan	GRAPHIC MODES:	480 x 200
YEAR:	1985	SIZE:	13.0 x 10.5 x 3.5"
CPU:	Motorola Mc 6800	WEIGHT:	8.0 #
SPEED:	8 MHZ	KEYBOARD:	76 Keys
RAM:	64 KB	POWER SUPPLY:	Ni-CD Battery Cells
ROM:	128 KB	PRICE:	450000 yens (Japan)
DISPLAY:	LCD	UNUSUAL FEATURES:	Many!!

Bondwell B2

Nothing is known about this scarce laptop except the following specs.

No Image Available

Rarity Scale: Rare

MANUFACTURER:	Bondwell	TEXT MODES:	16 Line x 80 Character
ORGIN:	UK/Hong Kong	GRAPHIC MODES:	640 x 200
YEAR	1985	SIZE:	11.0x12.5x3.0"
CPU:	Zilog Z80	WEIGHT:	12.1#
SPEED:	2.0MHZ	KEYBOARD:	77 Keys
RAM:	64K	POWER SUPPLY:	AC Adapter w/battery
ROM:	4K	PRICE:	$995.00
DISPLAY:	Mono LCD	UNUSUAL FEATURES:	None

Bull "L'Attache"

The L'Attache was Bull's first laptop computer to be produced. It was to be sold to the French Public Services as they were expected to buy French made computers. This was unusual since it was manufactured in Japan, not in France. The L'Attache had limited success in public sales due to other laptops being more innovative and lower priced.

Rarity scale: Rare

MANUFACTURER:	Bull Corporation	TEXT MODES:	25 Line x 80 Character
ORGIN	Japan	GRAPHIC MODES:	640 x 400
YEAR:	1987	SIZE:	13.0x13.0x3.5"
CPU:	8C286	WEIGHT:	12.0#
SPEED:	4.77Mhz)	KEYBOARD:	84 Keys
RAM:	640K	POWER SUPPLY:	AC Adapter w/battery
ROM:	Bios Rom	PRICE:	Unk
DISPLAY:	Mono LCD	UNUSUAL FEATURES:	None

Commodore LCD

This was one of the rarest Commodores ever built. It was not called the C64 Laptop! Commodore developed this 5 # machine and unveiled it at an electronic show in January 1985. It contained one of the best displays available at the time. This is a very rare laptop.

No Image Available

:

Rarity Scale: Rare

MANUFACTURER:	Commodore	TEXT MODES:	16 Line x 80 Character
ORGIN:	US	GRAPHIC MODES:	480 x 128
YEAR:	1985	SIZE:	11.0x11.75x2.2"
CPU:	Rockwell 65C102	WEIGHT:	5 #
SPEED:	1-2 Mhz	KEYBOARD:	Full Stroke
RAM:	32 KB	POWER SUPPLY:	4 Dry Cell Batteries
ROM:	96 KB	PRICE:	Unk
DISPLAY:	LCD	UNUSUAL FEATURES:	Built in Modem

Data General One

The Data General One was released as one of the first DOS based laptops to hit the market. It was not terribly heavy or bulky. Overall, it was a pretty nice laptop and continues to be very scarce.

No Image Available

Rarity: Rare

MANUFACTURER:	Data General	TEXT MODES:	28 Line x 80 Character
ORGIN:	US	GRAPHIC MODES:	640 x 256
YEAR:	1984	SIZE:	11.3x13.5x3.0"
CPU:	8088	WEIGHT:	9.0#
SPEED:	4.0MHZ	KEYBOARD:	79 Keys
RAM:	128K	POWER SUPPLY:	AC Adapter w/battery
ROM:	32K	PRICE:	$2895.00
DISPLAY:	Mono LCD	UNUSUAL FEATURES:	28 Line Display

Epson PX-16

When Epson introduced the PX-16 they already had a long history of portable computers, including the HX-20, PX-4, and the PX-8. This laptop is unusual in that it doesn't feature a hard drive or floppy drive, but has a RAM disk for storage. This was not much better than earlier models.

No Image Available

Rarity Scale: Rare

MANUFACTURER:	Epson Corp	TEXT MODES:	16 Line x 80 Character
ORGIN:	Japan/US	GRAPHIC MODE:	240 x 64
YEAR:	1988	SIZE:	Unk
CPU:	NEC V20	WEIGHT:	Unk
SPEED:	4.77MHZ	KEYBOARD:	80 Keys
RAM:	64K	POWER SUPPLY:	AC Adapter w/battery
ROM:	96K	PRICE:	Unk
DISPLAY:	Mono LCD	UNUSUAL FEATURES:	None

Epson Q150A

Nothing is known about this laptop except the listed specifications. I would consider it a crossover between a laptop and a portable. This is another of the very rare computers.

No Image Available

Rarity Scale: Rare

MANUFACTURER:	Epson Corp	TEXT MODE:	25 Line x 80 Character
ORGIN:	US/Japan	GRAPHIC MODE:	640 x 200
YEAR:	1989	KEYBOARD:	Unk
CPU:	8088	SIZE:	12x13.5x4.0"
SPEED:	4.77/10.0 MHZ	WEIGHT:	18.0#
RAM:	32K	POWER SUPPLY:	AC Adapter/battery
ROM:	Unk	PRICE:	Unk
DISPLAY:	MONO CGA	UNUSUAL FEATURES:	None

Fujitsu 16 FM Pi

Nothing is known about this except it was the laptop version of the Fujitsu FM16 Beta computer.

No Image Available

:

Rarity Scale: Rare

MANUFACTURER:	Fujitsu	TEXT MODES:	25 line X 80 Character
ORGIN:	Japan	GRAPHIC MODES:	640 x 200
YEAR:	1985	SIZE:	Unk
CPU:	8086/Zilog Z-80	WEIGHT:	Unk
SPEED:	5.0 Mhz	KEYBOARD:	Unk
RAM:	128K	POWER SUPPLY:	Unk
ROM:	Unk	PRICE:	Unk
DISPLAY:	LCD	UNUSUAL FEATURES:	Dual Processors

MicroOffice "Roadrunner"

This laptop was basically sold to OEMs and companies with heavy computer usage. They would not be sold through your regular computer store. However, a few may have been marketed through retail outlets under another name. The "Roadrunner" is a very rare machine.

No Image Available

Rarity Scale: Rare

MANUFACTURER:	MicroOffice	TEXT MODES:	8 Line x 80 Character
ORGIN:	US	GRAPHIC MODE:	64 x 480
YEAR:	1983	SIZE:	11.5x7.8x3.0"
CPU:	Zilog Z80A	WEIGHT:	5.0#
SPEED:	2.15MHZ	KEYBOARD:	73 Keys
RAM:	48K	POWER SUPPLY:	AC Adapter w/battery
ROM:	16K	PRICE:	$1695.00
DISPLAY:	Mono LCD	UNUSUAL FEATURES:	None

NEC PC-8500

A much needed improvement over the PC-8201A. It ran CP/M as the operating system. Nothing more is known about this sweet looking little laptop.

No Image available

Rarity Scale: Rare

MANUFACTURER:	NEC Corp	TEXT MODES:	25 Line x 80 Character
ORGIN:	Japan/US	GRAPHIC MODES:	Unk
YEAR:	1984	SIZE:	Unk
CPU:	Unk	WEIGHT:	Unk
SPEED:	Unk	KEYBOARD:	67 Keys
RAM:	64K	POWER SUPPLY:	Unk
ROM:	Unk	PRICE:	Unk
DISPLAY:	Mono LCD	UNUSUAL FEATURES:	Unk

Psion MC 200

This was one of three laptops manufactured by Psion in 1989. The MC 200 like the MC 400 and MC 600 did not sell well, Psion later denied this series of laptops ever existed!

No Image Available

Rarity Scale: Rare

MANUFACTURER:	Psion	TEXT MODES:	16 Line x 80 Character
ORGIN:	UK	GRAPHIC MODES:	640 x 400
YEAR:	1989	SIZE:	8.9x12.4x2.0"
CPU:	8086	WEIGHT:	4.3#
SPEED:	7.68MHZ	KEYBOARD:	Querty 63 Keys
RAM:	128K	POWER SUPPLY:	AC Adapter w/battery
ROM:	256K	PRICE:	595 UK#
DISPLAY:	Supertwist LCD	UNUSAL FEATURES:	None

Sharp PC-2500

This "A4" type laptop had the same characteristics as the Sharp1350 Pocket Computer but had a larger and much nicer keyboard. It also contained a small built-in color printer which was another popular feature. Unfortunately this unit had very little market success.

Rarity Scale: Rare

MANUFACTURER:	Sharp Corp	TEXT MODES:	4 Line x 24 Character
ORGIN:	US	GRAPHIC MODES:	150 x 32
YEAR:	1984	SIZE:	8.4x11.6x2.0"
CPU:	SC 61860	WEIGHT:	2.8#
SPEED:	Unk	KEYBOARD:	76 Keys
RAM:	3K	POWER SUPPLY:	Dry Cell Batteries
ROM:	72K	PRICE:	$370.00 (Est)
DISPLAY:	Mono LCD	UNUSUAL FEATURES:	Built in Printer

Sord IS 11

This was a compact laptop made in Japan, mostly for Japanese use. It featured a micro cassette recorder for data storage. The operating system used in this laptop was very difficult to learn. It was followed by the IS 11B & 11C into the market place.

Rarity Scale: Rare

MANUFACTURER:	Sord Corp	TEXT MODES:	8 Line x 40 Character
ORGIN:	Japan	GRAPHIC MODE:	256 x 44
YEAR:	1983	SIZE:	11.7x8.5x2.0"
CPU:	Zilog 80A	WEIGHT:	4.4#
SPEED:	3.4MHZ	KEYBOARD:	Querty 72 Key
RAM:	32K	POWER SUPPLY:	AC Adapter or Batteries
ROM:	64K	PRICE:	$995.00
DISPLAY:	Mono LCD	UNUSUAL FEATURES:	None

Sord 1S 11C

This was Sord's first laptop manufactured with a "clamshell "display which was a very big improvement. The1S 11 was also made in Japan for local use. It featured a micro cassette recorder instead of a disc drive which was used for data storage. Little else is known about it. This was the successor to the 1S 11.

Rarity Scale: Rare

MANUFACTURER:	Sord Corp	TEXT MODES:	25 Line x 80 Character
ORGIN:	Japan	GRAPHIC MODES:	640 x 200
YEAR:	1985	SIZE:	12.2x9.5x2.6"
CPU:	Zilog Z80A	WEIGHT:	6.6#
SPEED:	3.4MHZ	KEYBOARD:	Querty 72 Key
RAM:	80K	POWER SUPPLY:	AC Adapter w/battery
ROM:	144K	PRICE:	$1495.00
DISPLAY:	Mono LCD	UNUSUAL FEATURES:	None

Teleram T-3000

When the T-3000 was made available to users in 1982 it had the largest display being installed on laptops. This machine featured "true word processing" and used bubble memory which was a very scarce feature. This is a very rare laptop, few exist.

No Image Available

Rarity Scale: Rare

MANUFACTURER:	Teleram	TEXT MODES:	4 Line x 80 Character
ORGIN:	US	GRAPHIC MODE:	Unk
YEAR:	1982	SIZE:	13.0x9.0x3.5"
CPU:	Zilog Z80	WEIGHT:	9.0#
SPEED:	4.0MHZ	KEYBOARD:	83 Keys
RAM:	64K	POWER SUPPLY:	AC Adapter
ROM:	4K	PRICE:	$2995.00
DISPLAY:	Mono LCD	UNUSUAL FEATURES:	Bubble Memory

Texas Instruments "Pro Lite"

Nothing except the following specifications is known about this laptop. This computer is extremely scarce.

No Image Available

Rarity Scale: Rare

MANUFACTURER:	Texas Instruments	TEXT MODES:	25 Line x 80 Character
ORGIN:	US	GRAPHIC MODE:	640 x 200
YEAR	1985	SIZE:	Unk
CPU:	8088	WEIGHT:	Unk
SPEED:	5.0MHZ	KEYBOARD:	Unk
RAM:	256K	POWER SUPPLY:	AC Adapter
ROM:	32K	PRICE:	$2995.00
DISPLAY:	Mono LCD	UNUSUAL FEATURES:	None

Zenith Z-150A

Another of the Zenith laptops manufactured during the 1980s. Nothing except the following specifications is known about it.

No Image Available

Rarity Scale: Rare

MANUFACTURER:	Zenith Corp	TEXT MODES:	25 Line x 80 Character
ORGIN:	US	GRAPHIC MODES:	640 x 240
YEAR:	1984	SIZE:	Unk
CPU:	8C88	WEIGHT:	Unk
SPEED:	4.77MHZ	KEYBOARD:	94 Keys
RAM:	640K	POWER SUPPLY:	AC Adapter w/battery
ROM:	Unk	PRICE:	Unk
DISPLAY:	Mono LCD	UNUSUAL FEATURES:	None

Epilogue

It is remarkable that of all the different types of personal computers designed and produced during the 1980s, only 2 survived into the 1990's, the "Clamshell" Laptop, and the Desktop. There was another type that hung on a little while into the 1990s- the "A4" laptop. It occurred to me following the turbulent 80s as things settled down somewhat, that time and effort seemed to be spent developing and refining the 2 surviving types. There were new items being designed but nothing as dramatic as the earlier era. Not until after the turn of the century did things appear to get out of hand again. Now there are new devices being designed daily. It has reached the point, by the time a computer or other device has been built and sold, it has already been deemed obsolete, as newer, faster, or smaller units have replaced it. The new trend is moving toward mini or micro computers or related items taking the spotlight. I have absolutely no knowledge of what is in the market place now, if I did, I would have no idea what to do with it!! I guess you would say "I am mired in the 90s". Is this the beginning of the end of the personal computers we enjoyed during the 1990s?? How I long for the old days when we were not bombarded by ads, pop ups, and "spam" every time we went online, when we were not forced to install virus scans, pop up-blockers, and firewalls, etc. It used to be fun to "surf the net" when we needed a little information or just wanted to waste a bit of time. Now there seems to be a constant intrusion of spam interrupting our every move. I am beginning to wonder if it is worth the stress to do it. Also as with most people, I am appalled at the evil some internet users are exposing our younger generation to.

The direction the industry is heading is scary to me as computers are now controlling all phases of our daily lives. Computers were designed to help us live a better life and have enhanced our existence in countless ways. Now they are intruding upon our privacy in countless ways also.

If for some catastrophic reason our country's computer systems cease to operate-- airplanes would not be allowed to fly, banks could not conduct business, cash registers would cease to function, electric grids would power down, our military communication could be in chaos, etc. The whole country would go dark and the business world would grind to a standstill. Frightening, isn't it??

When will the "powers-that-be" begin addressing the above mentioned subjects? Security, usability, and dependability problems need to be recognized and updated. These should be more important issues than industry's madness in fueling this "out of control" technology race. It appears to me the technology sector has one thing in mind, the "bottom line". I believe the industry should focus their resources on safeguarding our existence which would be more beneficial to society than the way they are functioning today.

Twenty five years ago, a great technological advance came into being in the form of personal computers. To all beings of the earth we were given the ability to achieve great things. But we should never forget we were also given the tools to destroy our way of life if this technology is not used intelligently, and with great fore thought.

The above paragraph is one man's view of where we are heading.   Hopefully we have the incentive and desire, to correct our course to the future? If not..........